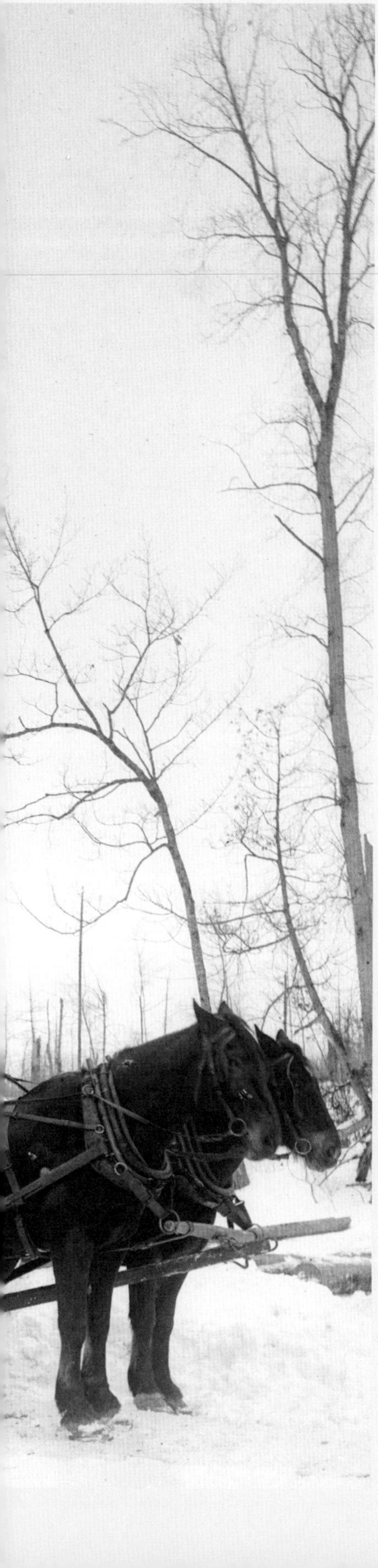

NOAH VAN SCIVER

T0002532

PAUL BUNYAN:
THE INVENTION OF AN AMERICAN LEGEND

With art and stories by
MARLENA MYLES

Introduction by
LEE FRANCIS IV

Postcript by
DEONDRE SMILES

A TOON GRAPHIC • NEW YORK

FOR EVERY CHILD WHO WAS DISPOSSESSED, FOR EVERY TREE THAT WAS FELLED, LET THEIR STORY BE KNOWN. — The authors

Joseph Bird Head, Dakota Indian, c. 1899 by Heyn Photo. Courtesy: Library of Congress.

For Remy and Amy — *NVS*

Editorial Direction and Book Design: FRANÇOISE MOULY

Executive Editor: TUCKER STONE

Endpapers: MARLENA MYLES

NOAH VAN SCIVER's artwork was drawn in India ink and colored digitally.

FOR VISUAL READERS
TOON GRAPHICS

A TOON Book™ © 2023 Noah Van Sciver & TOON Books, an imprint of Astra Books for Young Readers, a division of Astra Publishing House. Individual contributions © their respective authors. Copying or digitizing this book for storage, display, or distribution in any other medium is strictly prohibited. All rights reserved. For information about permission to reproduce selections from this book, please contact permissions@astrapublishinghouse.com. TOON Books®, TOON Graphics™, and TOON Into Reading!™ are trademarks of Astra Publishing House. Library of Congress Cataloging-in-Publication Data: Names: Van Sciver, Noah, author, illustrator. | Myles, Marlena, 1981- author, illustrator. Title: Paul Bunyan : the invention of an American legend / Noah Van Sciver; with stories and art by Marlena Myles ; introduction by Lee Francis IV; postscript by Deondre Smiles. Description: New York : Toon Books, 2023. | Series: A Toon graphic | Includes bibliographical references. | Audience: Ages 7+ | Audience: Grades 4-6 | Summary: "In a humorous graphic novel set in Minnesota around 1914, we see W. B. Laughead, an advertising manager for a lumber company, spin the Paul Bunyan tall tales. Highlights the impact of clear-cutting old-growth forests. With contributions by Native authors as well as historical maps, photos, and a bibliography."-- Provided by publisher. Identifiers: LCCN 2022053690 | ISBN 9781662665226 (hardcover) | ISBN 9781662665233 (paperback) | ISBN 9781662665240 (ebk) Subjects: LCSH: Bunyan, Paul (Legendary character)--Comic books, scripts, etc. | Logging--United States--History--Comic books, scripts, etc. | LCGFT: Graphic novels Classification: LCC GR105.37.P38 V36 2023 | DDC 398.21--dc23/eng/20221208 LC record available at https://lccn.loc.gov/2022053690. All our books are Smyth Sewn (the highest library-quality binding available) and printed with soy-based inks on acid-free, woodfree paper harvested from responsible sources. Printed in China. First edition.

ISBN 978-1-6626-6522-6 (hardcover)   ISBN 978-1-6626-6523-3 (paperback)

10 9 8 7 6 5 4 3 2 1

WWW.TOON-BOOKS.COM

THE POWER OF STORYTELLING

by Lee Francis IV

PUEBLO OF LAGUNA

People often ask me for advice on authentic and accurate books about Native peoples. My primary focus on all aspects of education in and around Indigenous and Native American communities in North America has always led me to advocate for all kinds of stories to be told. But what do you do when you find out that a story you loved as a kid is a tall tale spun by an advertising man intent on justifying the clear-cutting of our ancestral lands by lumber companies?

HULL RUST MINE
SCRANTON MINE
FUTURE SITE OF HIBBING MINN.
LAKE SUPERIOR

As a six-year-old Pueblo kid, I came to the Paul Bunyan story by way of a 1958 Disney cartoon, a Silly Symphony treatment of the oversized lumberjack and his blue ox. I found it delightful, and it helped cement my love of American culture. To be sure, all societies and nations have unique mythologies, but the feeling of being American is essentially built on myths. From Columbus to Pocahontas to Johnny Appleseed to John Henry, the American story is one in which history and fiction are woven together, often at the expense of marginalized groups.The character of Paul Bunyan was manufactured to help promote the timber industry, but its overarching theme is broader: it's the common colonial theme of settling various lands and regions that once belonged to Indigenous peoples to make way for "American civilization."

The original characters of Bunyan and Babe the Blue Ox were created around the 1910s by William B. Laughead (pronounced low-heed), an advertising man. Nowadays, many people imagine them the way they were portrayed in a 1958 Walt Disney short cartoon: Paul dropped the lumberjack's shirt, and the two of them became considerably cuter.

Many years later, I am still a fan of those old Disney cartoons, but I am now much more aware of the ways in which popular culture influences the collective consciousness. I see how, in America, the lines between commercial speech and folklore were often blurred in the country's quest to secure its fledgling identity and expand its global footprint. (At home, Bunyan seems to many like authentic Americana, and abroad, there's nothing more American than Mickey Mouse®.) But this "American" identity is often much too narrowly defined.

Stories and myths are essential for our sense of identity and community, but knowing the true origins of our stories, and unearthing the stories they replaced or eradicated, is the key to a truly inclusive American culture. If we continue to tell *all* our stories and also give readers the means to understand their creation and their impact, we can come closer to accepting the diversity of our heritage. And ultimately, it's only the acceptance of that diversity that can reveal the true strength of the American experience.

Clockwise from top left: Illustrated Hibbing souvenir postcard depicting Paul Bunyan and the Iron Range, c. 1950. *Courtesy: Minnesota Historical Society.* • *Photo of William B. Laughead. Courtesy: Kerlan Collection, University of Minnesota Libraries.* • Paul Bunyan *animation frame © Disney Corp. All rights reserved.*

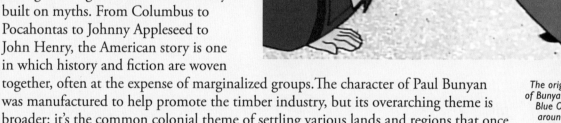

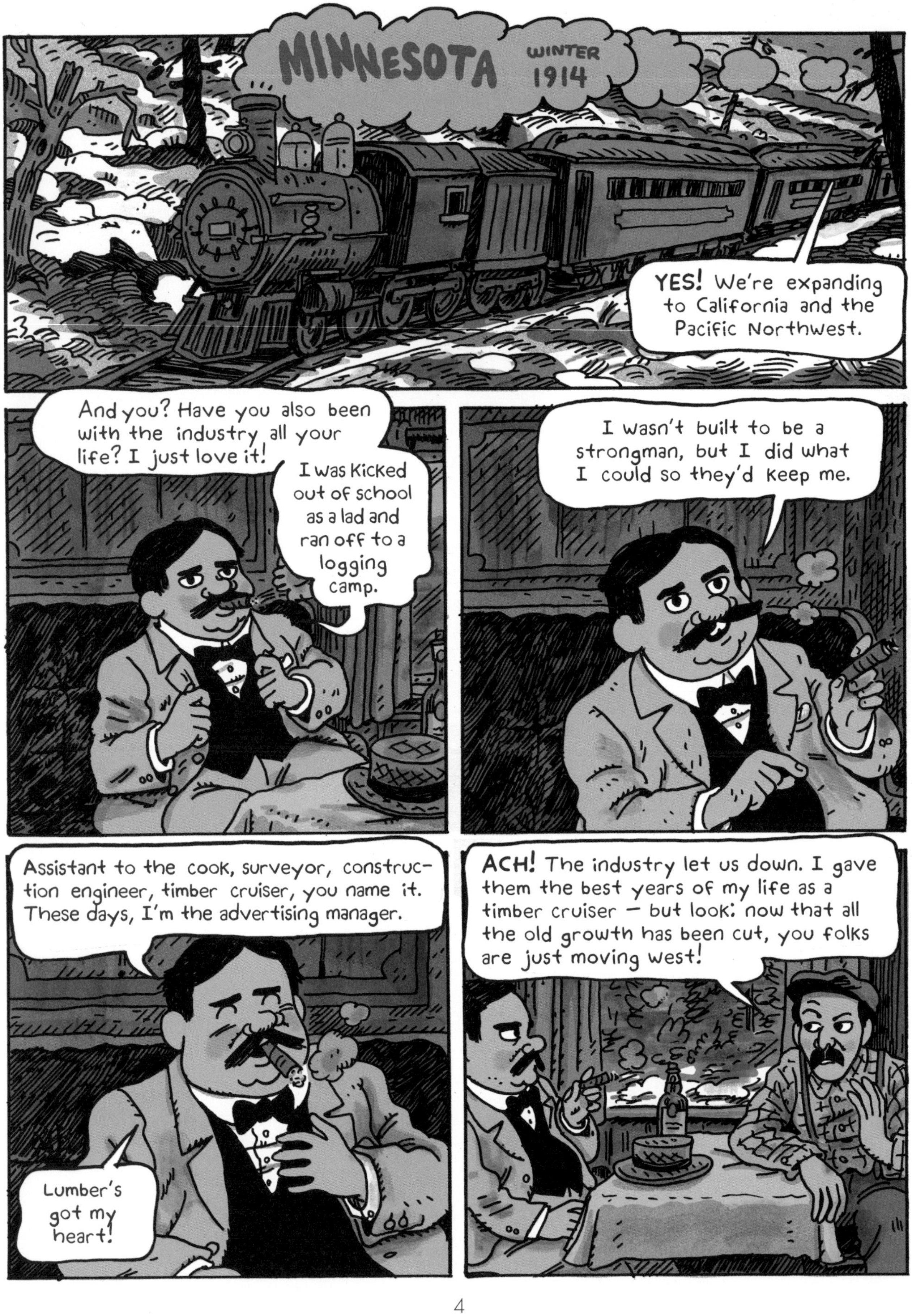
MINNESOTA WINTER 1914
YES! We're expanding to California and the Pacific Northwest.
And you? Have you also been with the industry all your life? I just love it!
I was Kicked out of school as a lad and ran off to a logging camp.
I wasn't built to be a strongman, but I did what I could so they'd keep me.
Assistant to the cook, surveyor, construction engineer, timber cruiser, you name it. These days, I'm the advertising manager.
Lumber's got my heart!
ACH! The industry let us down. I gave them the best years of my life as a timber cruiser — but look: now that all the old growth has been cut, you folks are just moving west!

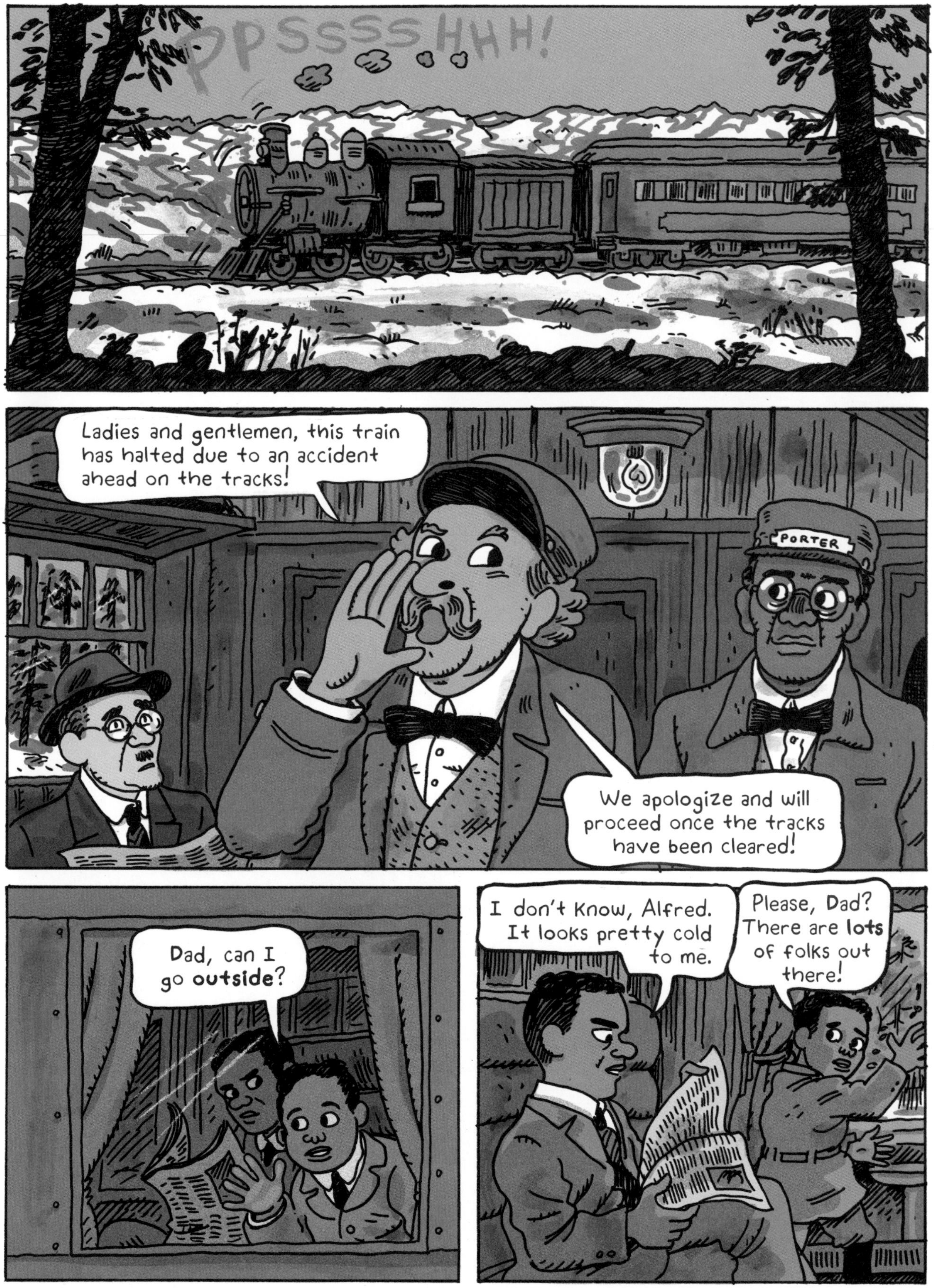
PPSSSSHHH!
Ladies and gentlemen, this train has halted due to an accident ahead on the tracks!
PORTER
We apologize and will proceed once the tracks have been cleared!
Dad, can I go **outside**?
I don't know, Alfred. It looks pretty cold to me.
Please, Dad? There are **lots** of folks out there!

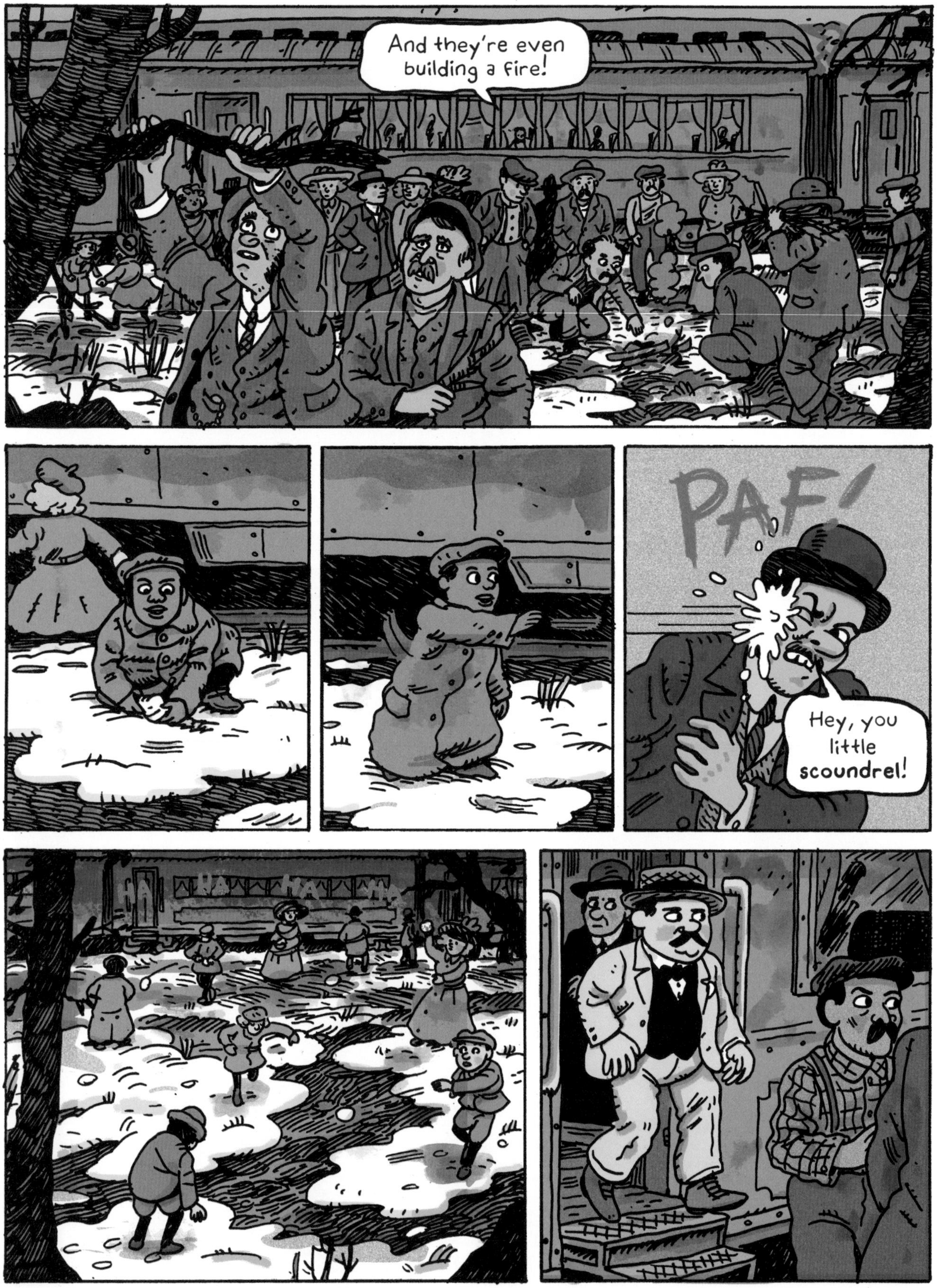
And they're even building a fire!
PAF!
Hey, you little scoundrel!
HA HA HA HA

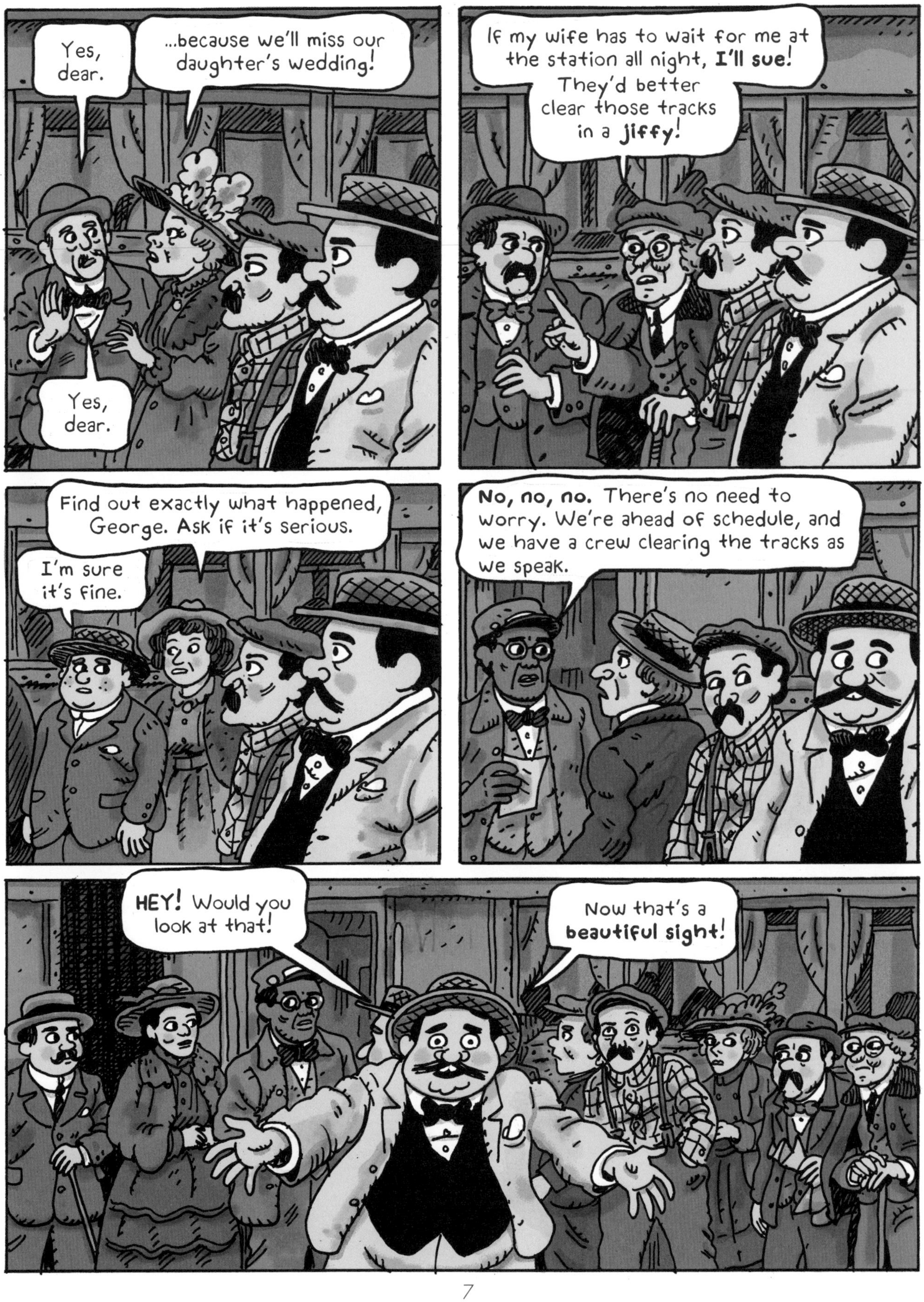

Yes, dear.
...because we'll miss our daughter's wedding!
Yes, dear.
If my wife has to wait for me at the station all night, **I'll sue!**
They'd better clear those tracks in a **jiffy!**
Find out exactly what happened, George. Ask if it's serious.
I'm sure it's fine.
No, no, no. There's no need to worry. We're ahead of schedule, and we have a crew clearing the tracks as we speak.
HEY! Would you look at that!
Now that's a **beautiful sight!**

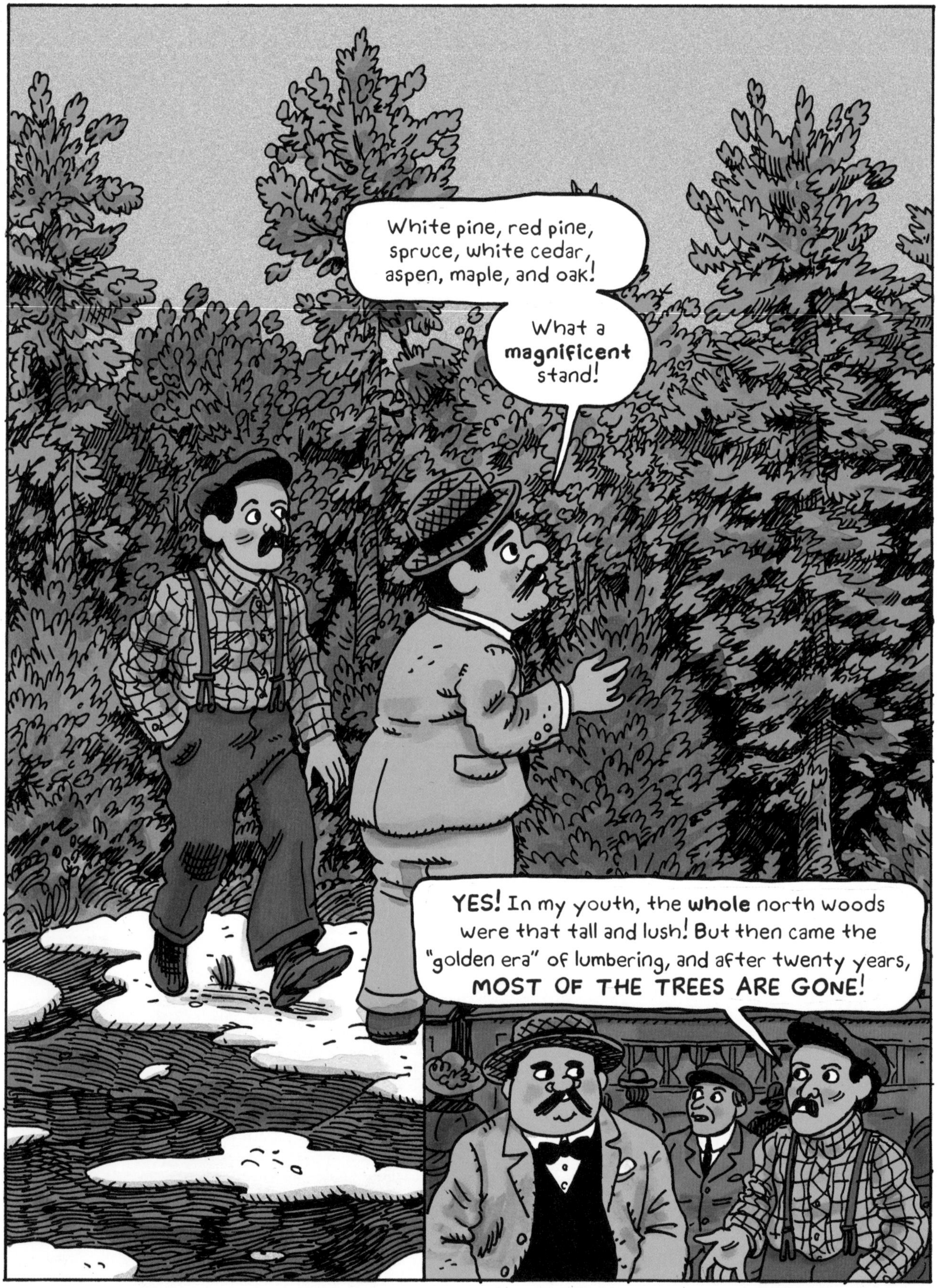
White pine, red pine, spruce, white cedar, aspen, maple, and oak!
What a **magnificent** stand!
YES! In my youth, the **whole** north woods were that tall and lush! But then came the "golden era" of lumbering, and after twenty years, **MOST OF THE TREES ARE GONE!**

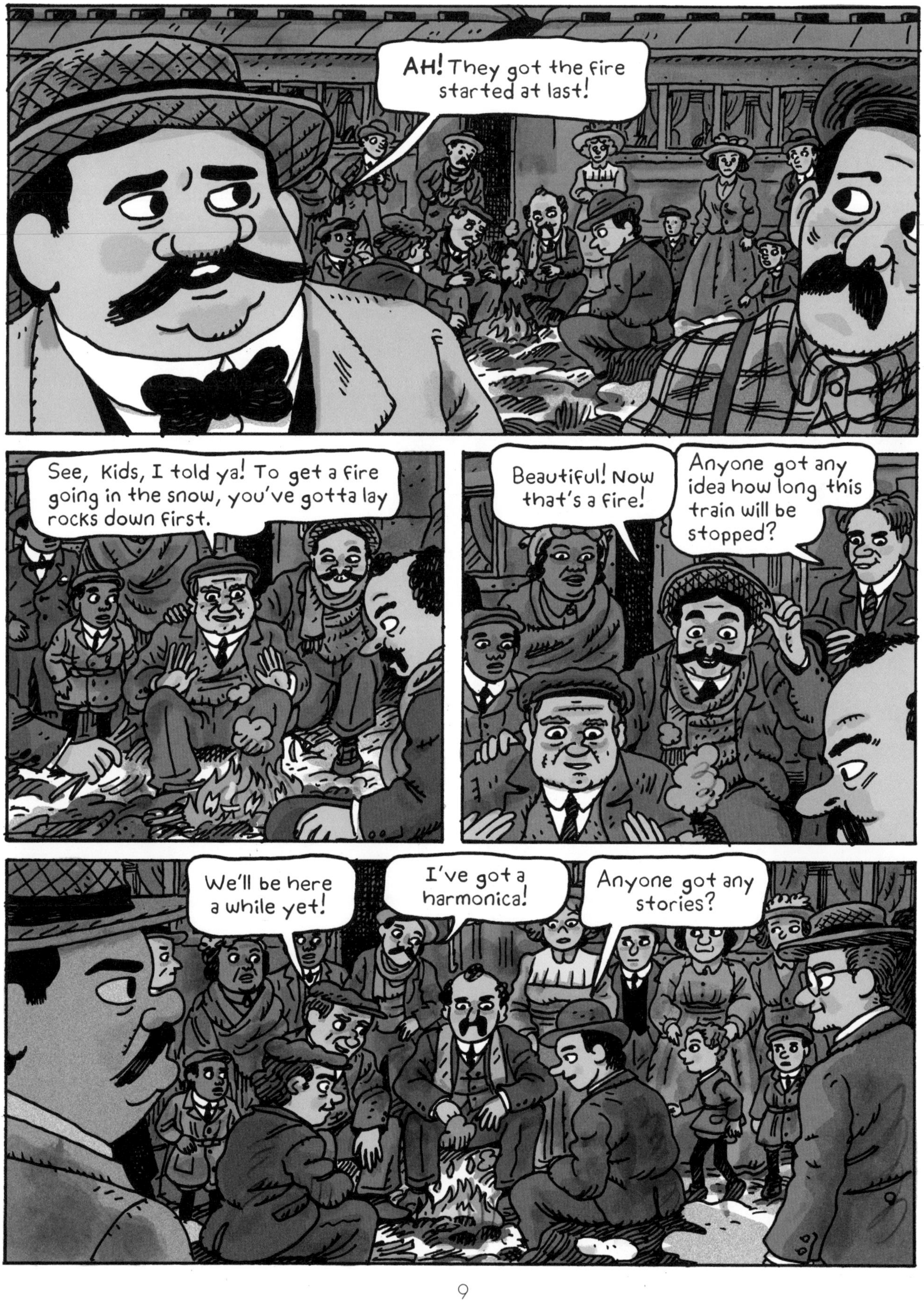
AH! They got the fire started at last!
See, Kids, I told ya! To get a fire going in the snow, you've gotta lay rocks down first.
Beautiful! Now that's a fire!
Anyone got any idea how long this train will be stopped?
We'll be here a while yet!
I've got a harmonica!
Anyone got any stories?

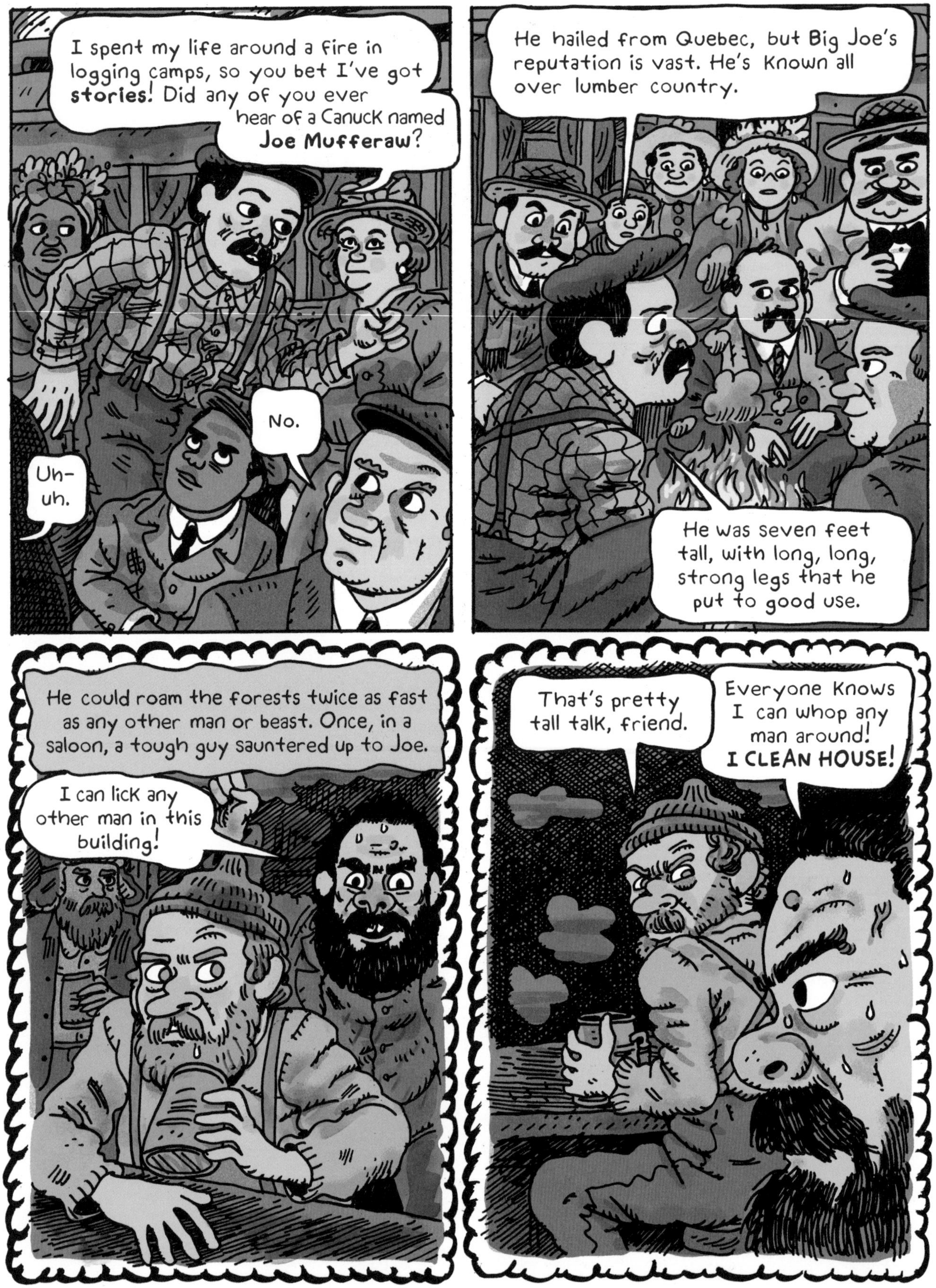
I spent my life around a fire in logging camps, so you bet I've got **stories**! Did any of you ever hear of a Canuck named **Joe Mufferaw**?
Uh-uh.
No.
He hailed from Quebec, but Big Joe's reputation is vast. He's known all over lumber country.
He was seven feet tall, with long, long, strong legs that he put to good use.
He could roam the forests twice as fast as any other man or beast. Once, in a saloon, a tough guy sauntered up to Joe.
I can lick any other man in this building!
That's pretty tall talk, friend.
Everyone knows I can whop any man around! **I CLEAN HOUSE!**

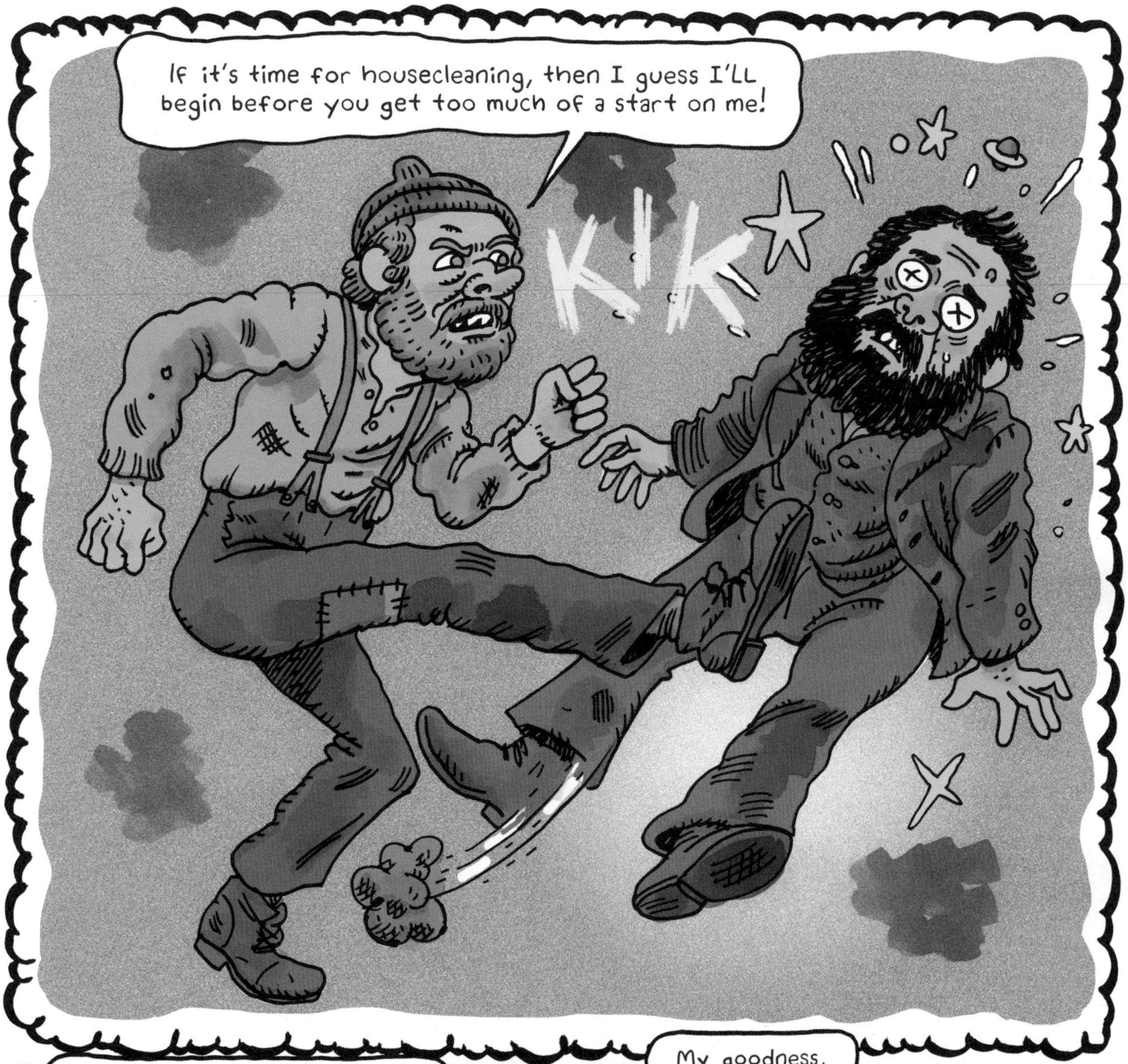
If it's time for housecleaning, then I guess I'LL begin before you get too much of a start on me!
KIK

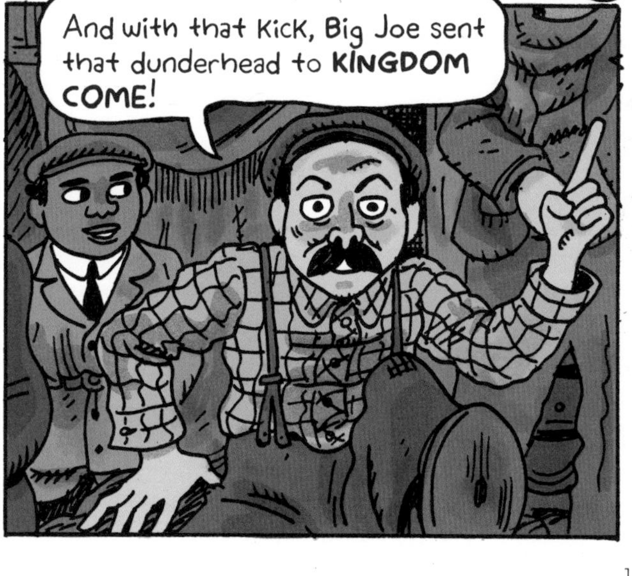
And with that kick, Big Joe sent that dunderhead to **KINGDOM COME!**

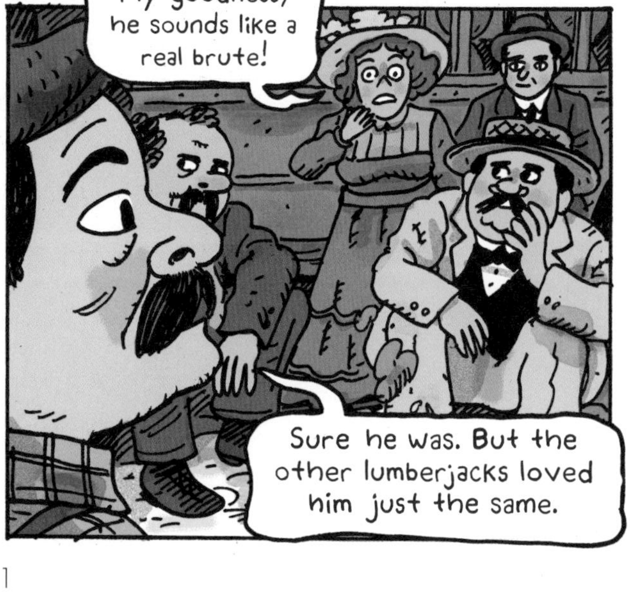
My goodness, he sounds like a real brute!
Sure he was. But the other lumberjacks loved him just the same.

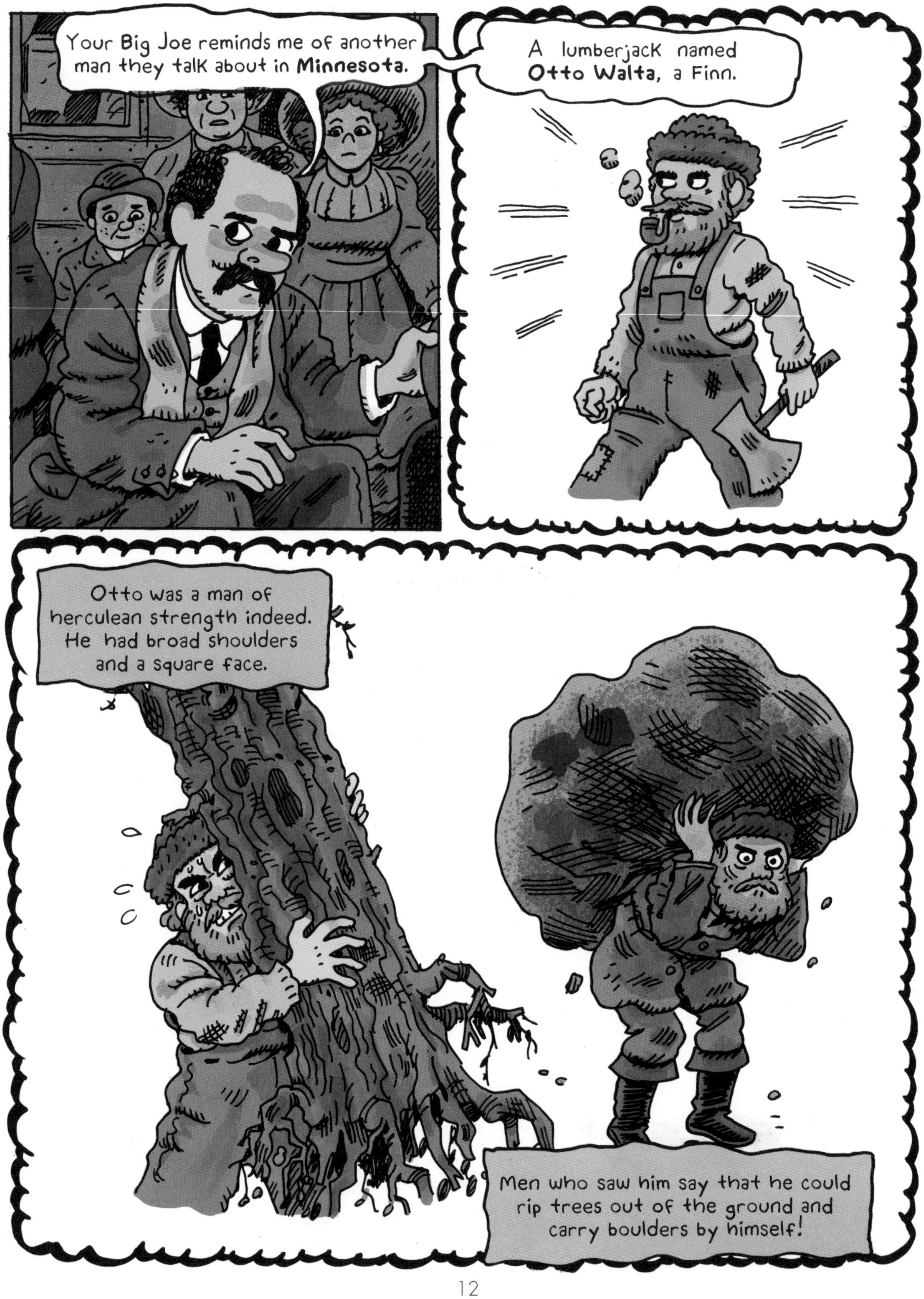

Your Big Joe reminds me of another man they talk about in Minnesota.
A lumberjack named Otto Walta, a Finn.
Otto was a man of herculean strength indeed. He had broad shoulders and a square face.
Men who saw him say that he could rip trees out of the ground and carry boulders by himself!

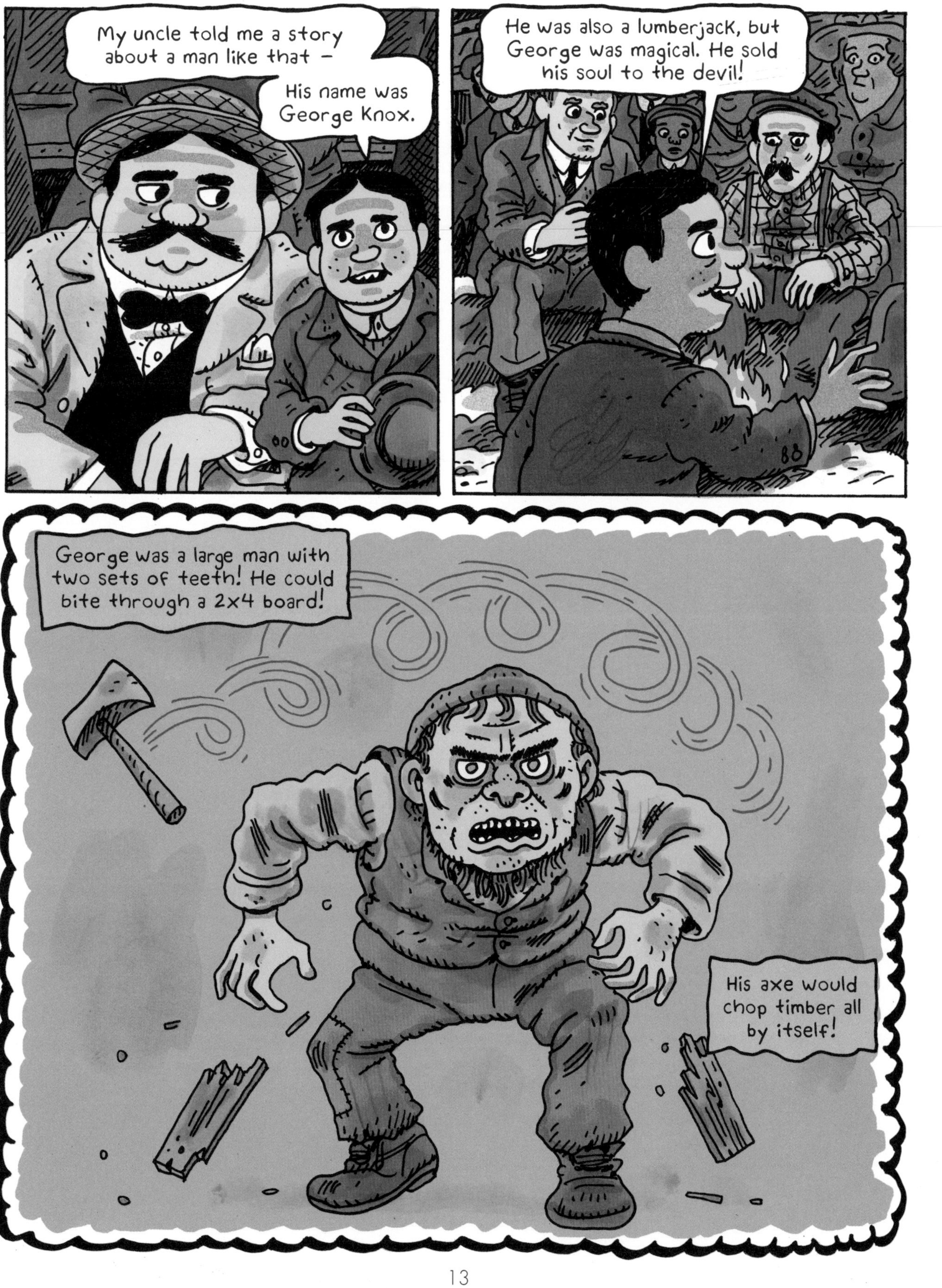
My uncle told me a story about a man like that –
His name was George Knox.
He was also a lumberjack, but George was magical. He sold his soul to the devil!
George was a large man with two sets of teeth! He could bite through a 2x4 board!
His axe would chop timber all by itself!

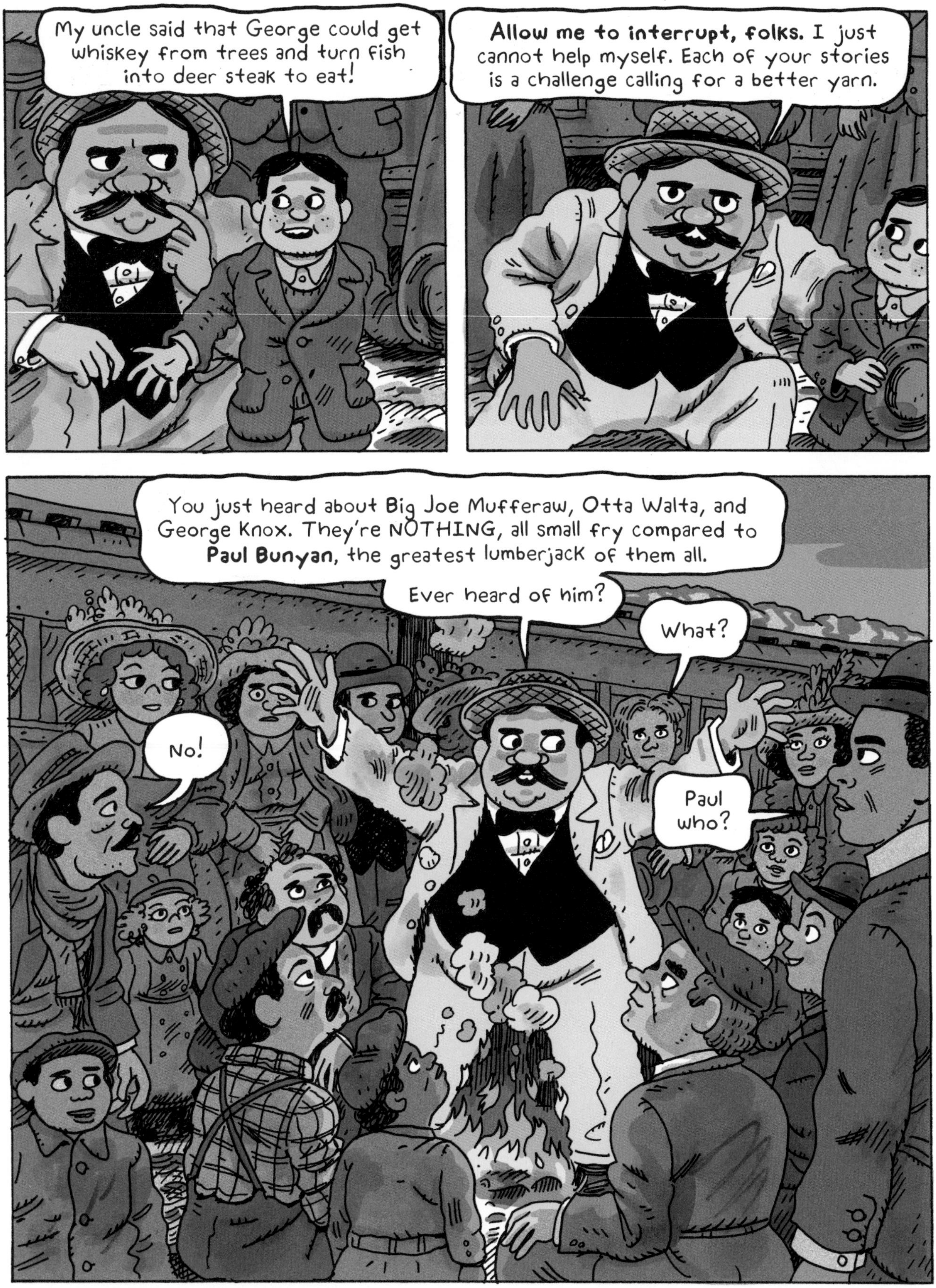
My uncle said that George could get whiskey from trees and turn fish into deer steak to eat!
Allow me to interrupt, folks. I just cannot help myself. Each of your stories is a challenge calling for a better yarn.
You just heard about **Big Joe Mufferaw, Otta Walta,** and **George Knox.** They're NOTHING, all small fry compared to **Paul Bunyan**, the greatest lumberjack of them all.
Ever heard of him?
No!
What?
Paul who?

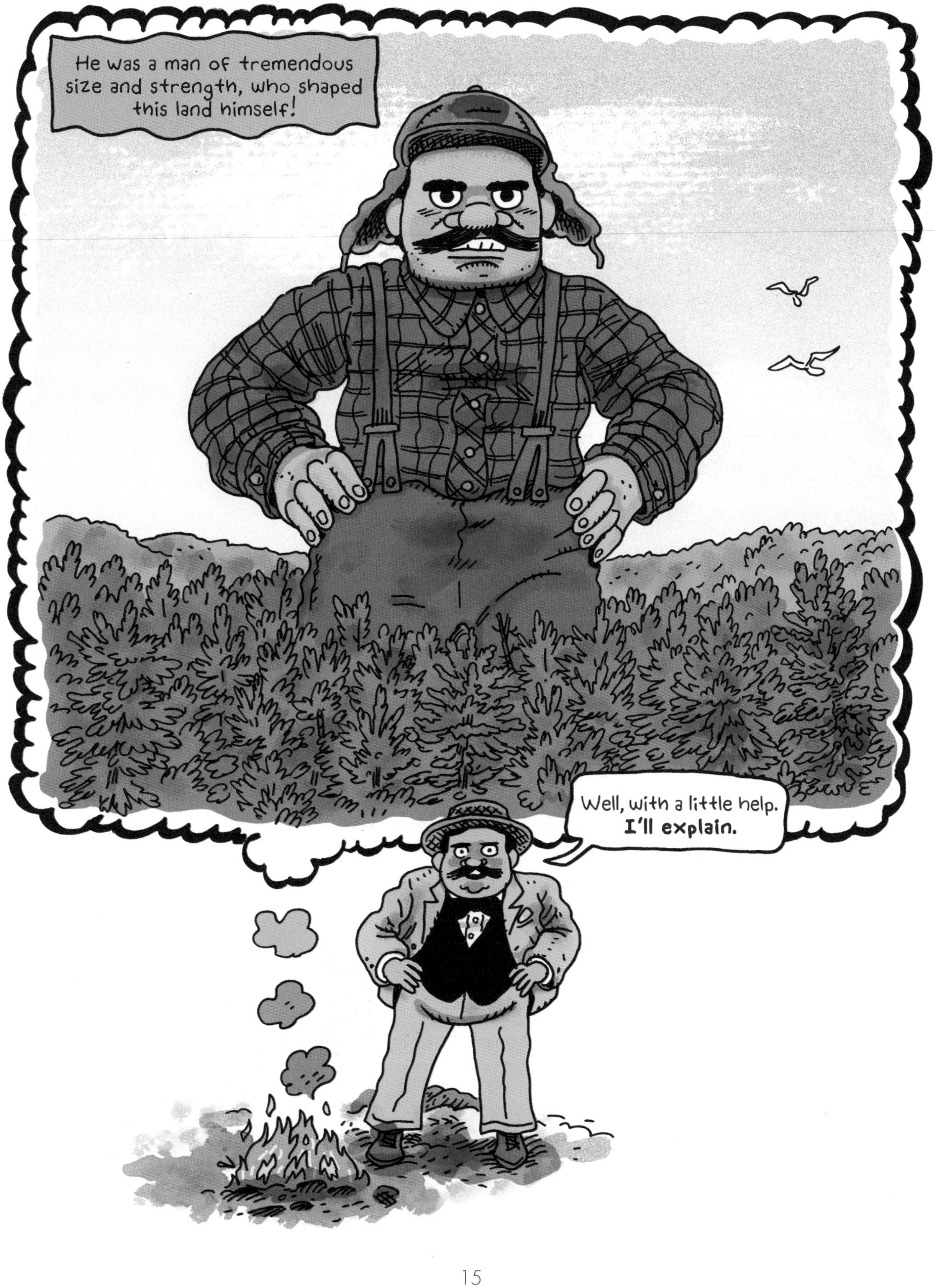
He was a man of tremendous size and strength, who shaped this land himself!
Well, with a little help. **I'll explain.**

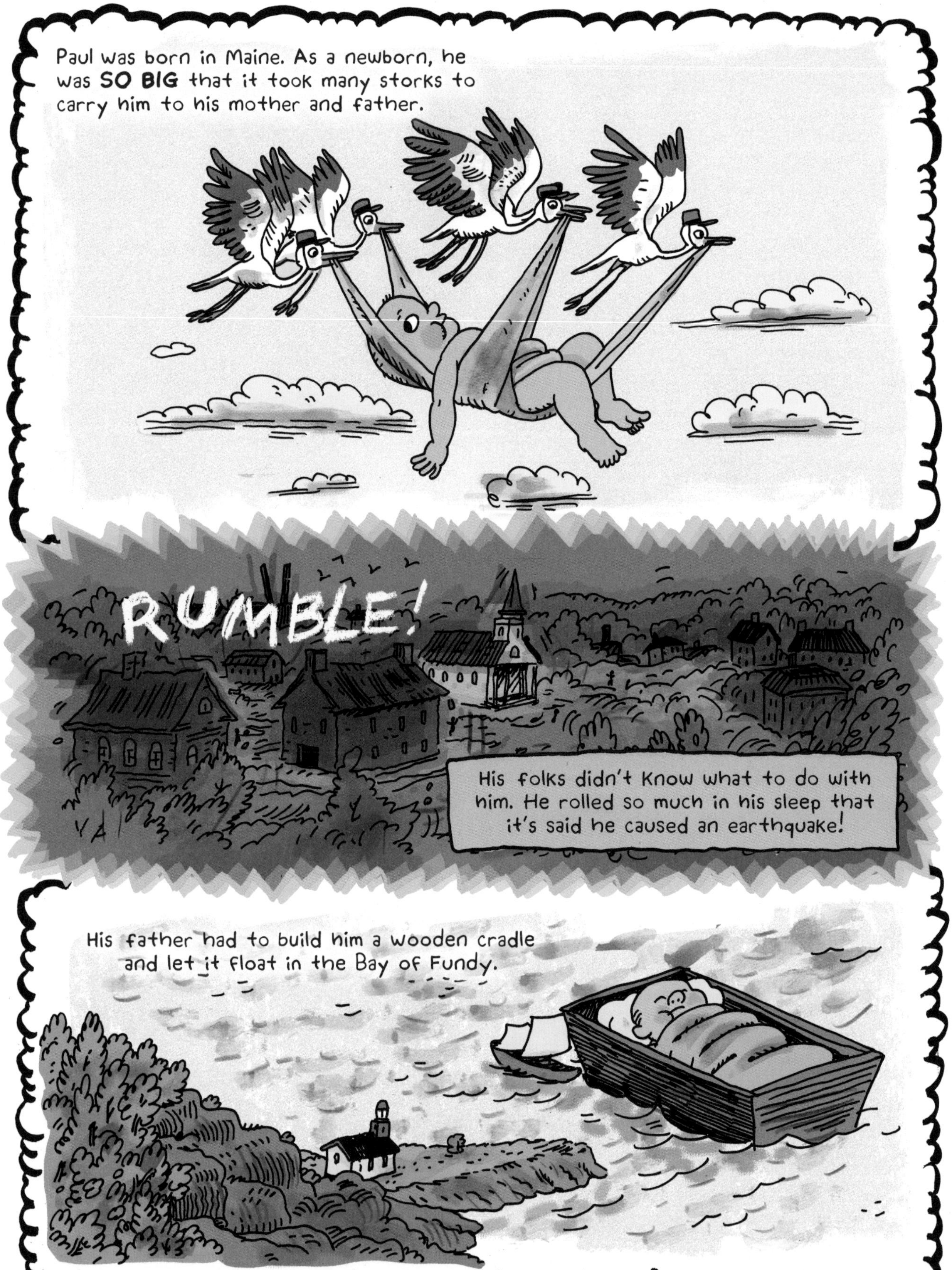
Paul was born in Maine. As a newborn, he was **SO BIG** that it took many storks to carry him to his mother and father.
RUMBLE!
His folks didn't know what to do with him. He rolled so much in his sleep that it's said he caused an earthquake!
His father had to build him a wooden cradle and let it float in the Bay of Fundy.

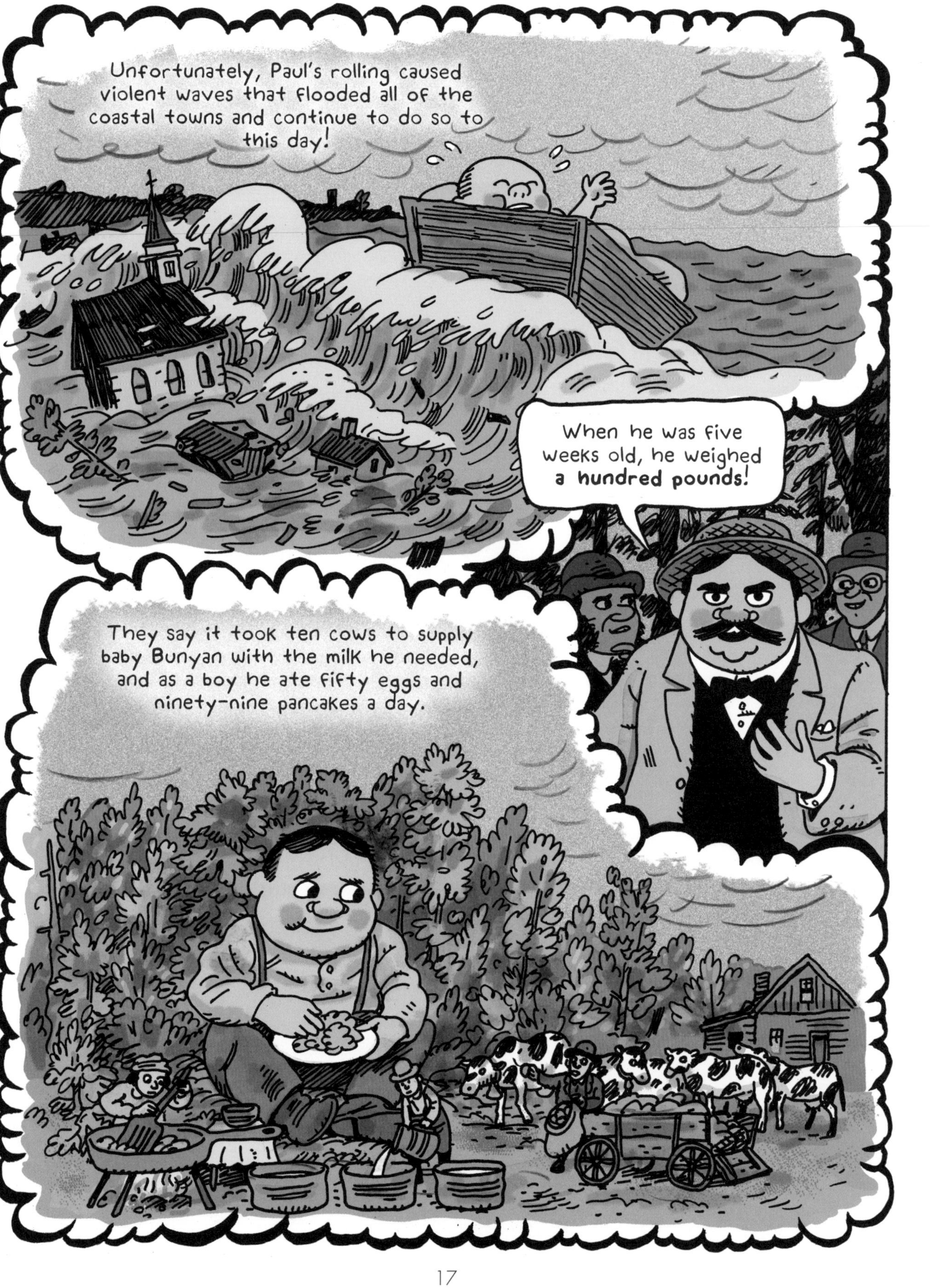
Unfortunately, Paul's rolling caused violent waves that flooded all of the coastal towns and continue to do so to this day!
When he was five weeks old, he weighed **a hundred pounds!**
They say it took ten cows to supply baby Bunyan with the milk he needed, and as a boy he ate fifty eggs and ninety-nine pancakes a day.

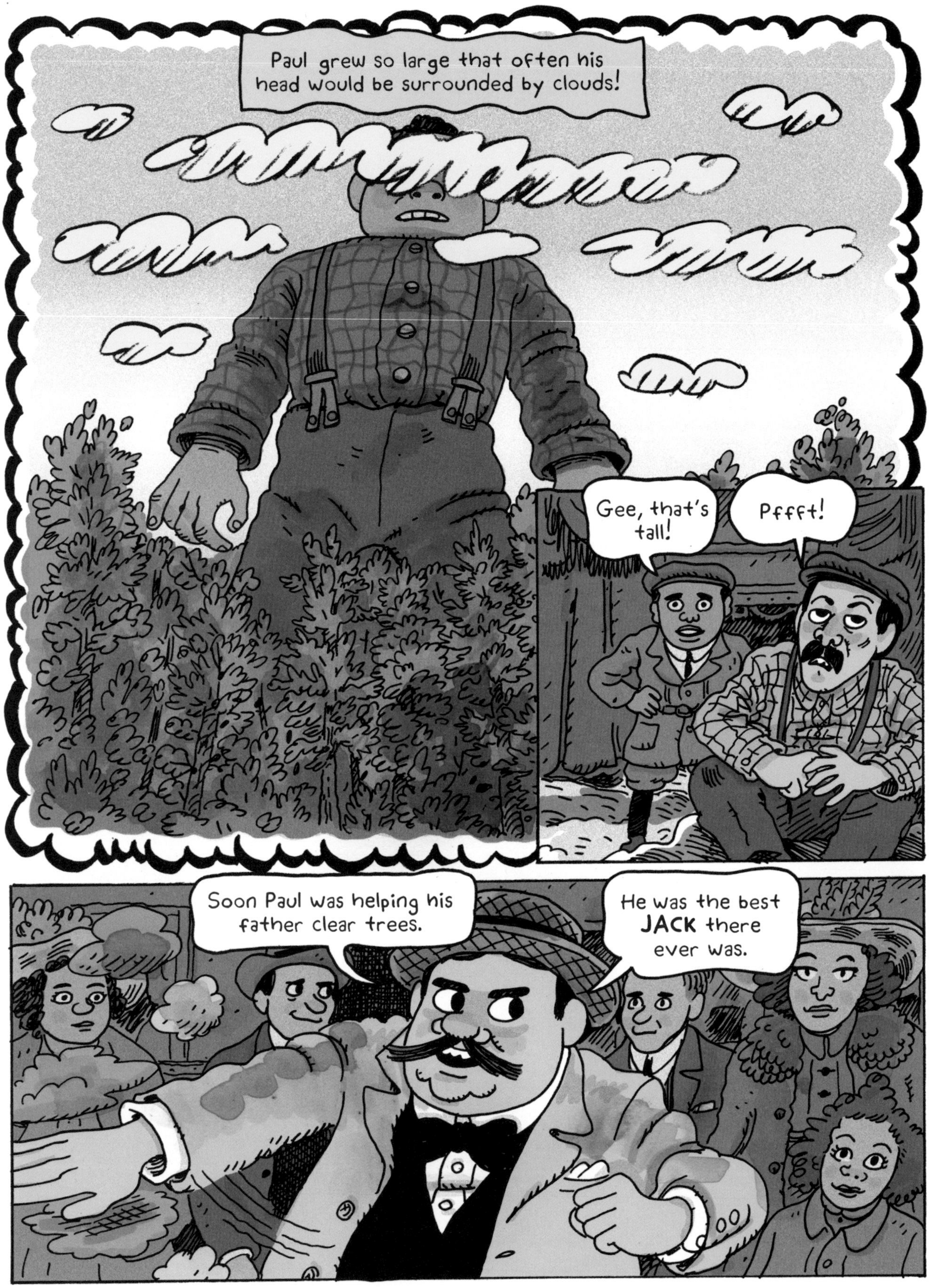
Paul grew so large that often his head would be surrounded by clouds!
Gee, that's tall!
Pffft!
Soon Paul was helping his father clear trees.
He was the best JACK there ever was.

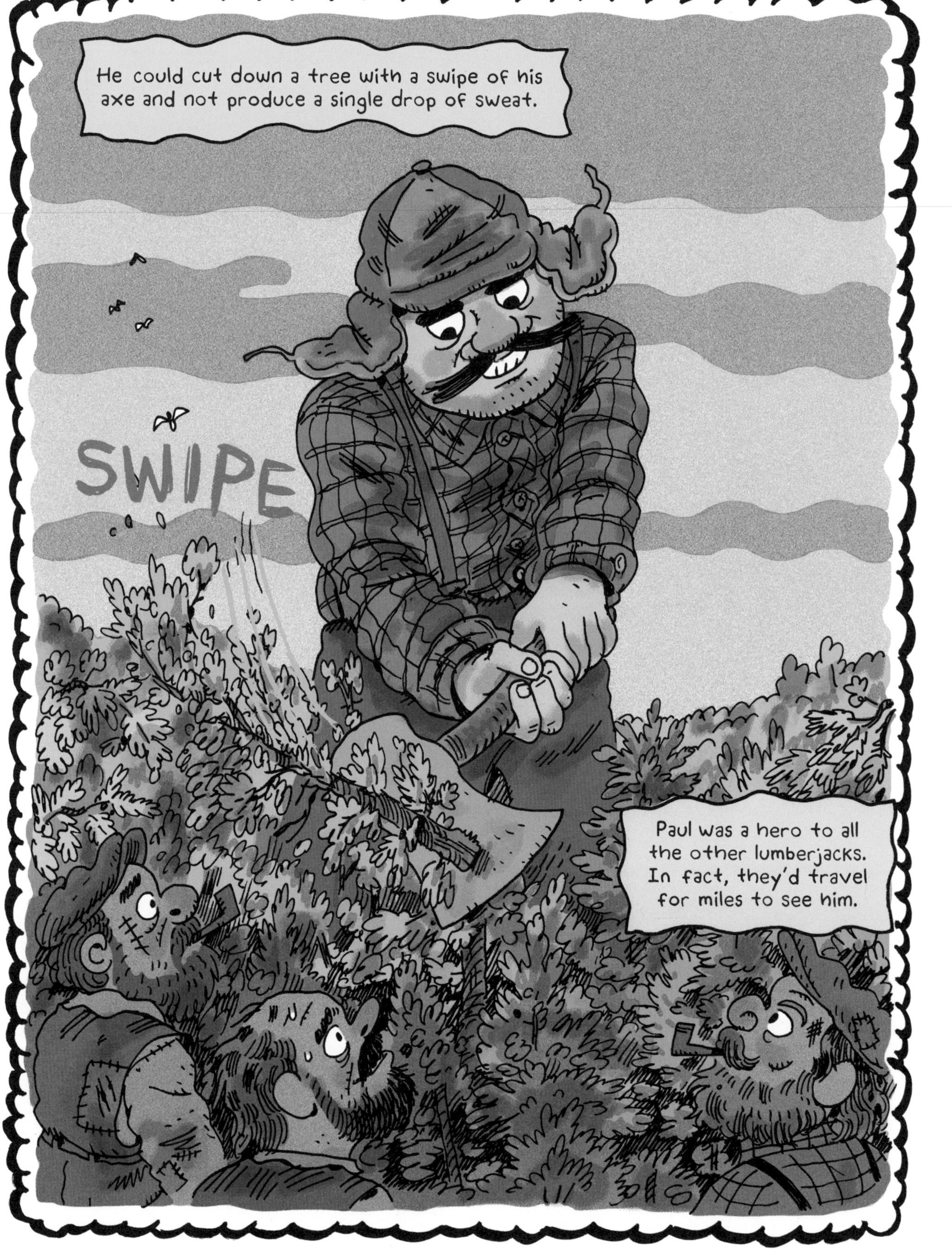
He could cut down a tree with a swipe of his axe and not produce a single drop of sweat.
SWIPE
Paul was a hero to all the other lumberjacks. In fact, they'd travel for miles to see him.

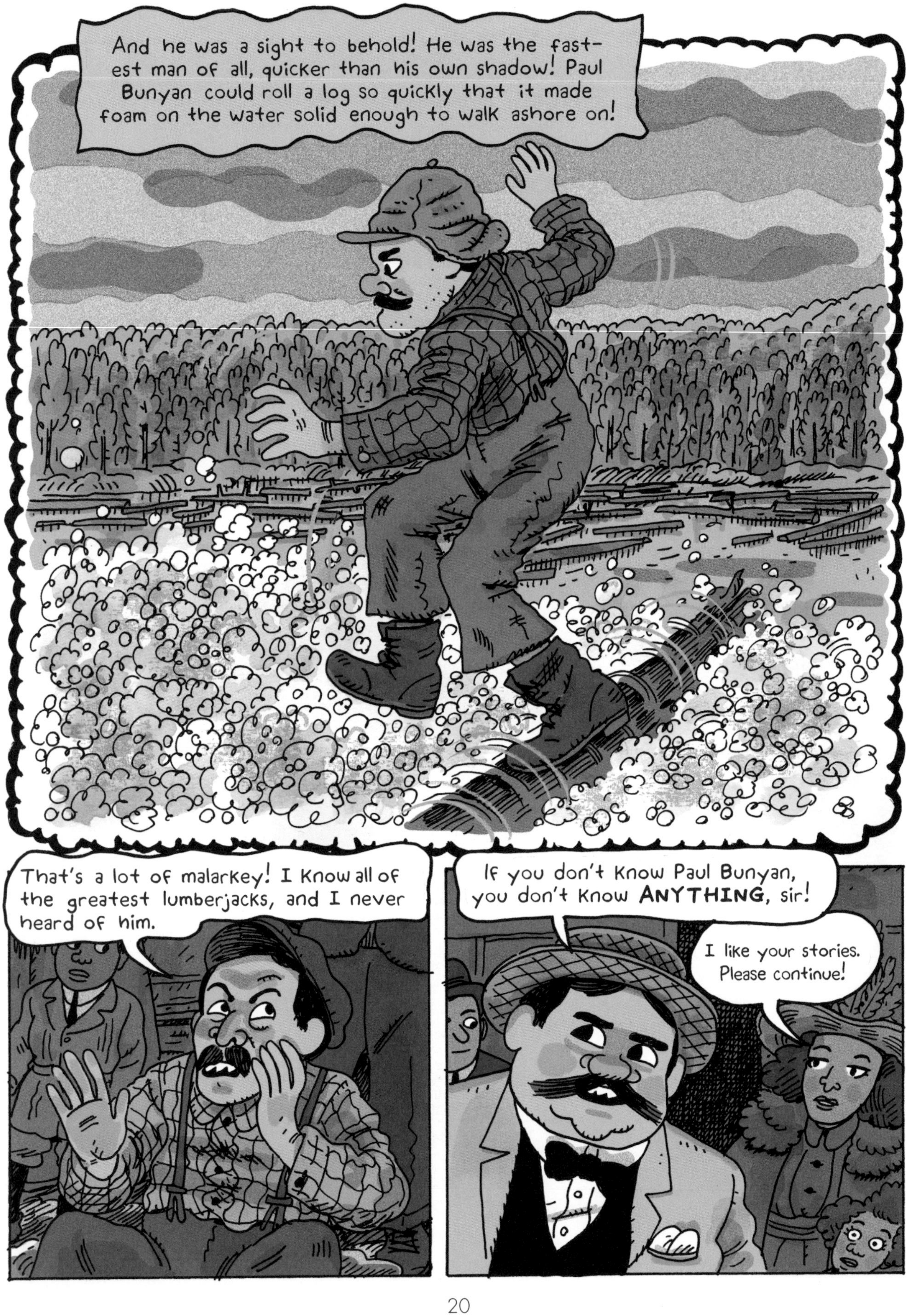
And he was a sight to behold! He was the fastest man of all, quicker than his own shadow! Paul Bunyan could roll a log so quickly that it made foam on the water solid enough to walk ashore on!
That's a lot of malarkey! I know all of the greatest lumberjacks, and I never heard of him.
If you don't know Paul Bunyan, you don't know ANYTHING, sir!
I like your stories. Please continue!

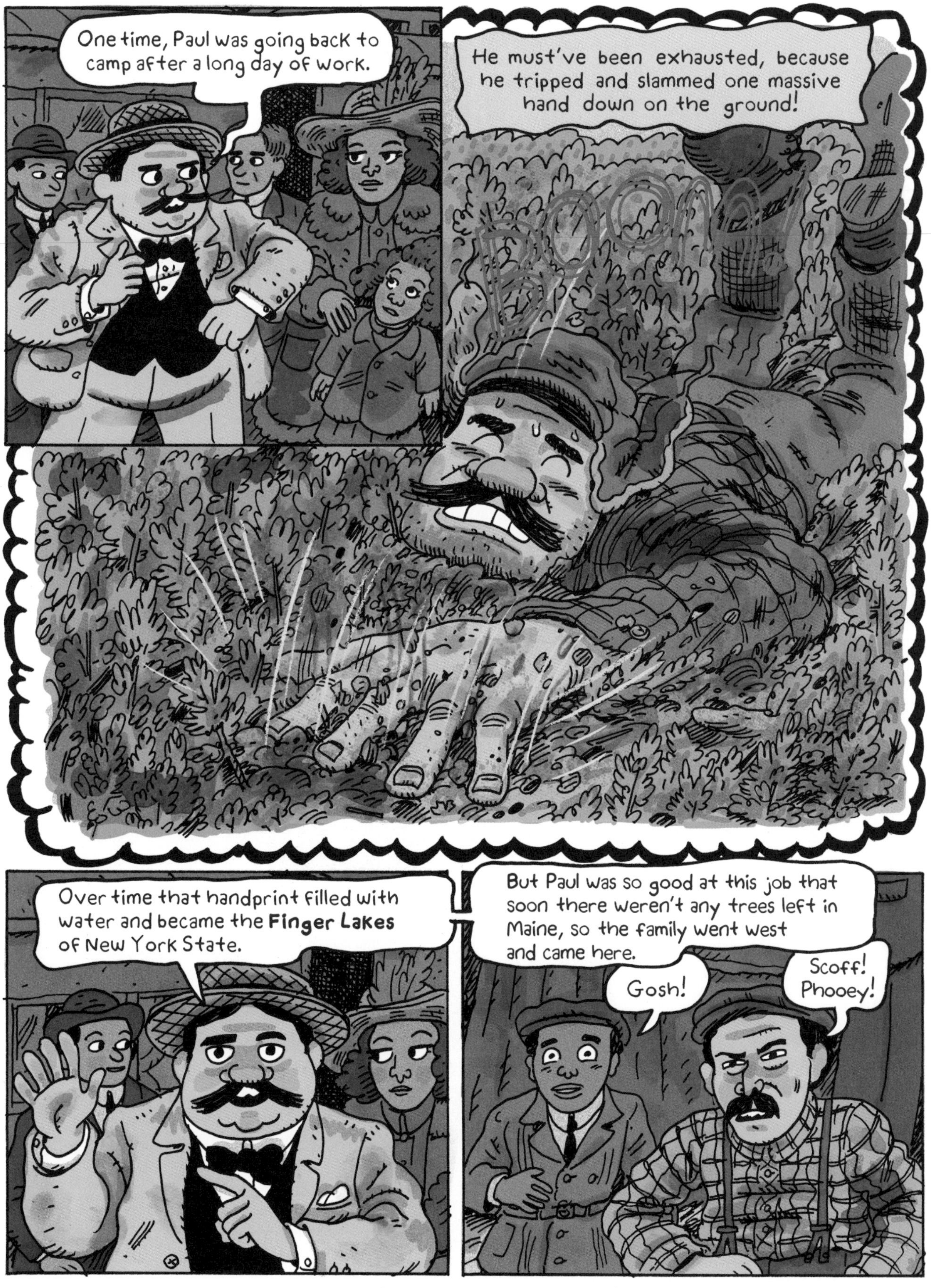
One time, Paul was going back to camp after a long day of work.
He must've been exhausted, because he tripped and slammed one massive hand down on the ground!
BOOM!
Over time that handprint filled with water and became the **Finger Lakes** of New York State.
But Paul was so good at this job that soon there weren't any trees left in Maine, so the family went west and came here.
Gosh!
Scoff! Phooey!

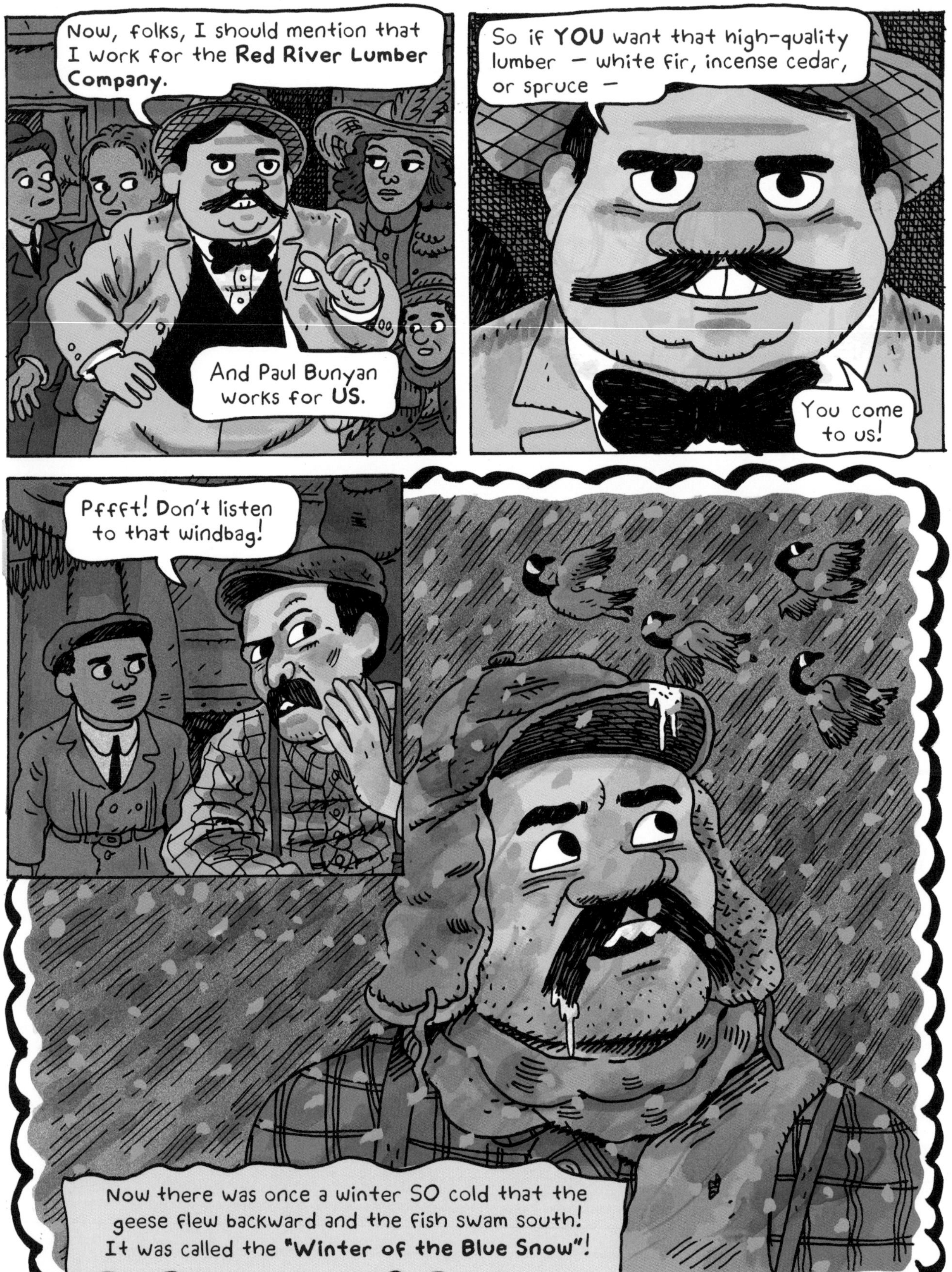

Now, folks, I should mention that I work for the **Red River Lumber Company.**
And Paul Bunyan works for **US.**
So if **YOU** want that high-quality lumber – white fir, incense cedar, or spruce –
You come to us!
Pfffft! Don't listen to that windbag!
Now there was once a winter SO cold that the geese flew backward and the fish swam south! It was called the **"Winter of the Blue Snow"!**

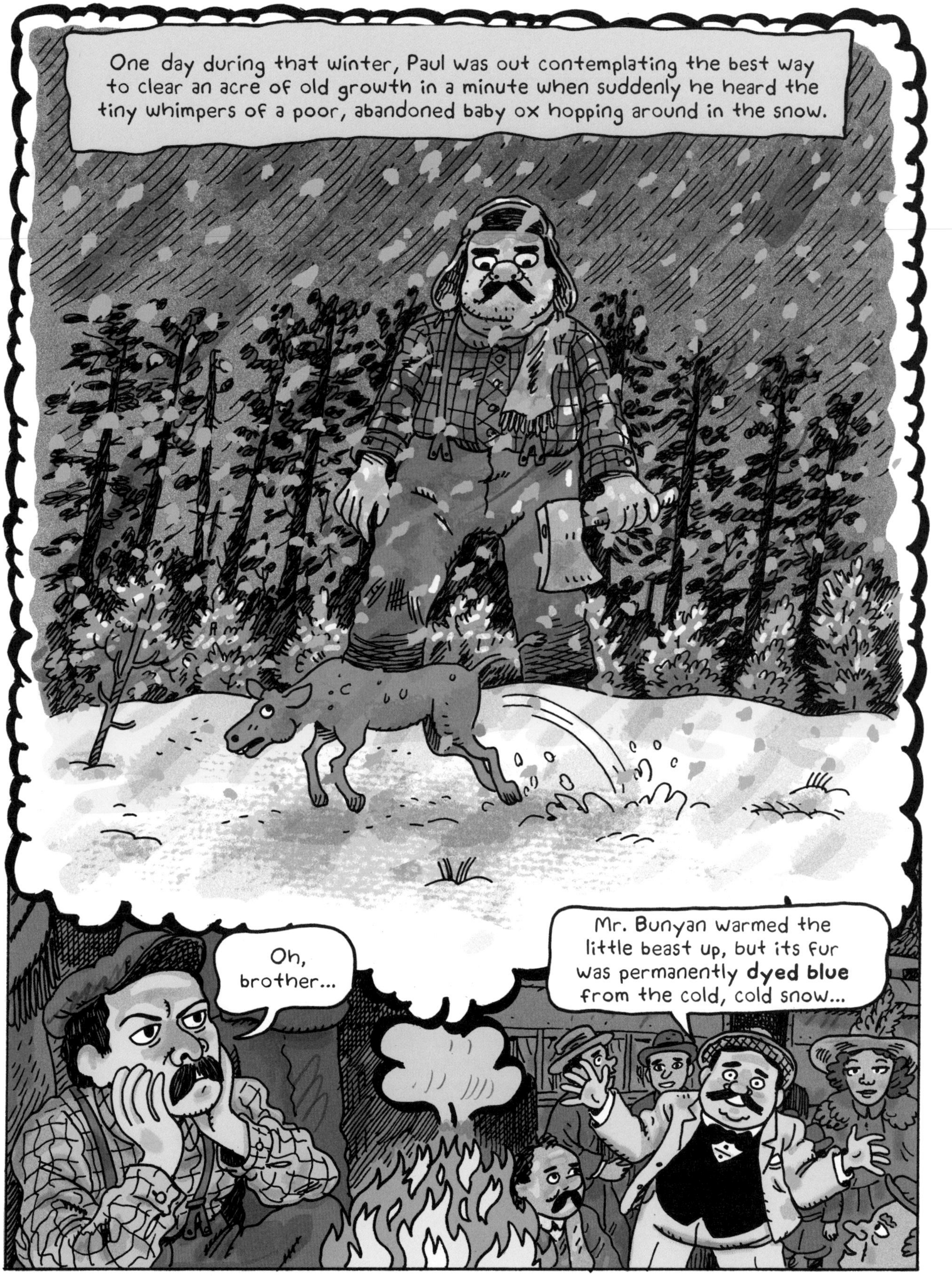
One day during that winter, Paul was out contemplating the best way to clear an acre of old growth in a minute when suddenly he heard the tiny whimpers of a poor, abandoned baby ox hopping around in the snow.
Oh, brother...
Mr. Bunyan warmed the little beast up, but its fur was permanently **dyed blue** from the cold, cold snow...

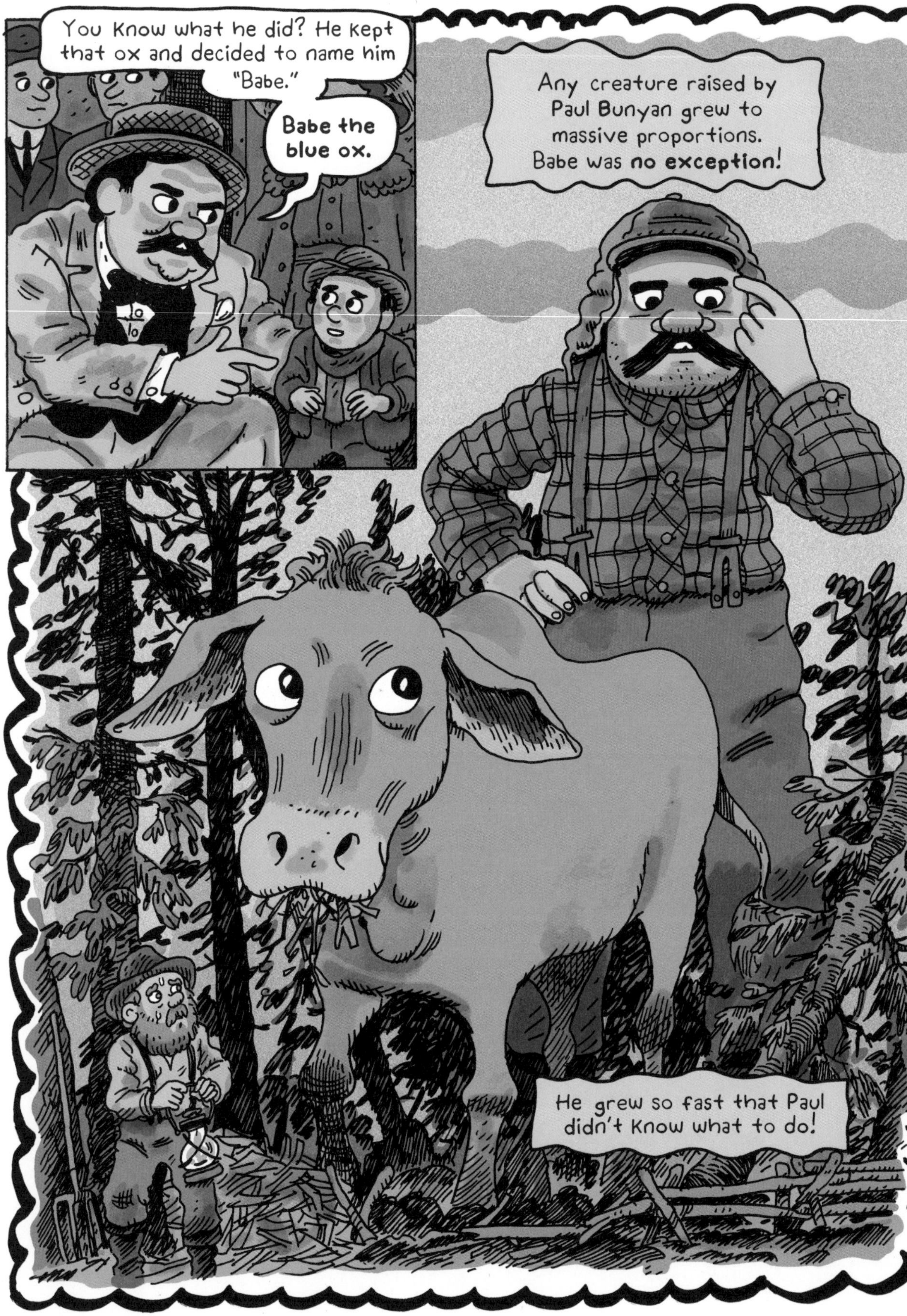
You know what he did? He kept that ox and decided to name him "Babe."
Babe the blue ox.
Any creature raised by Paul Bunyan grew to massive proportions. Babe was **no exception**!
He grew so fast that Paul didn't know what to do!

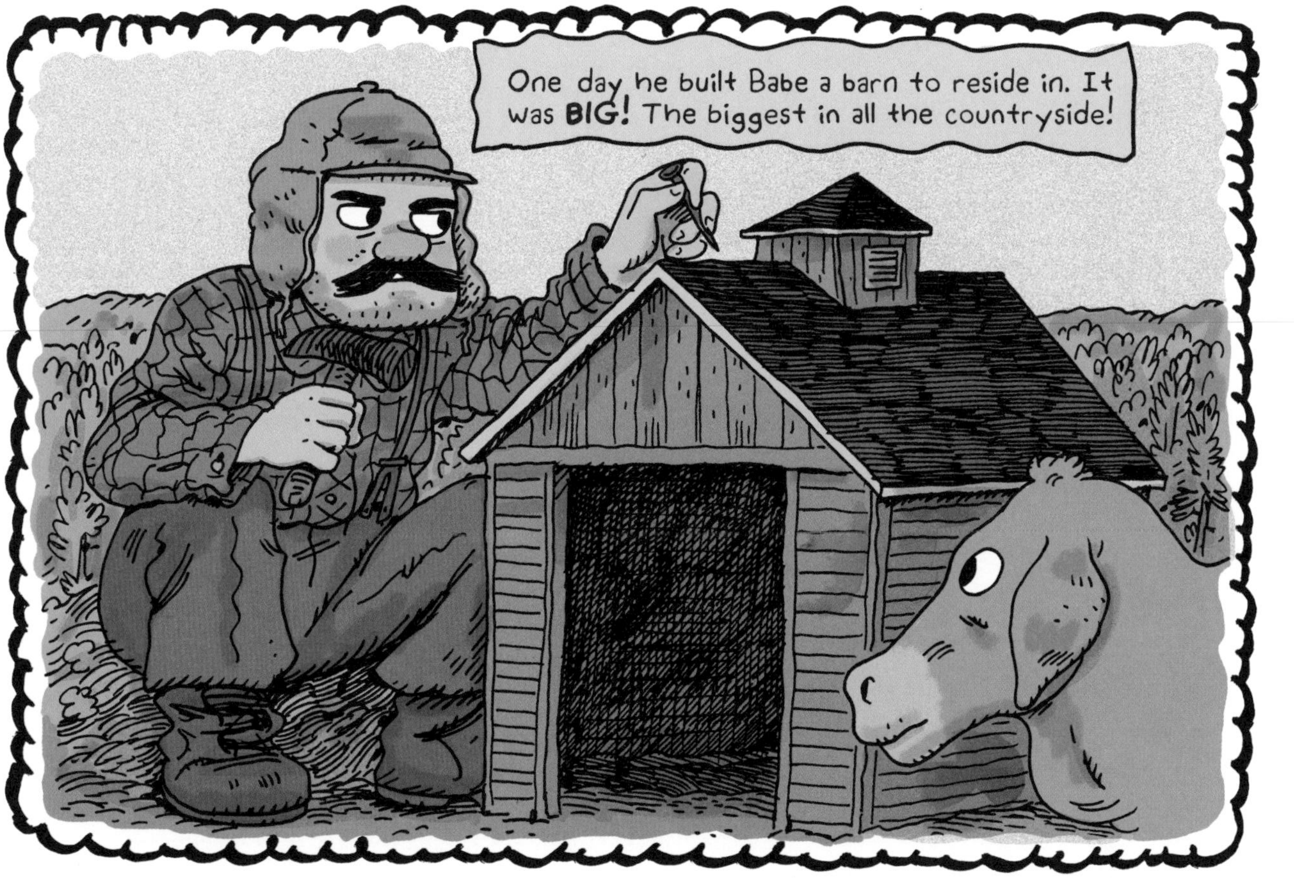
One day he built Babe a barn to reside in. It was **BIG!** The biggest in all the countryside!

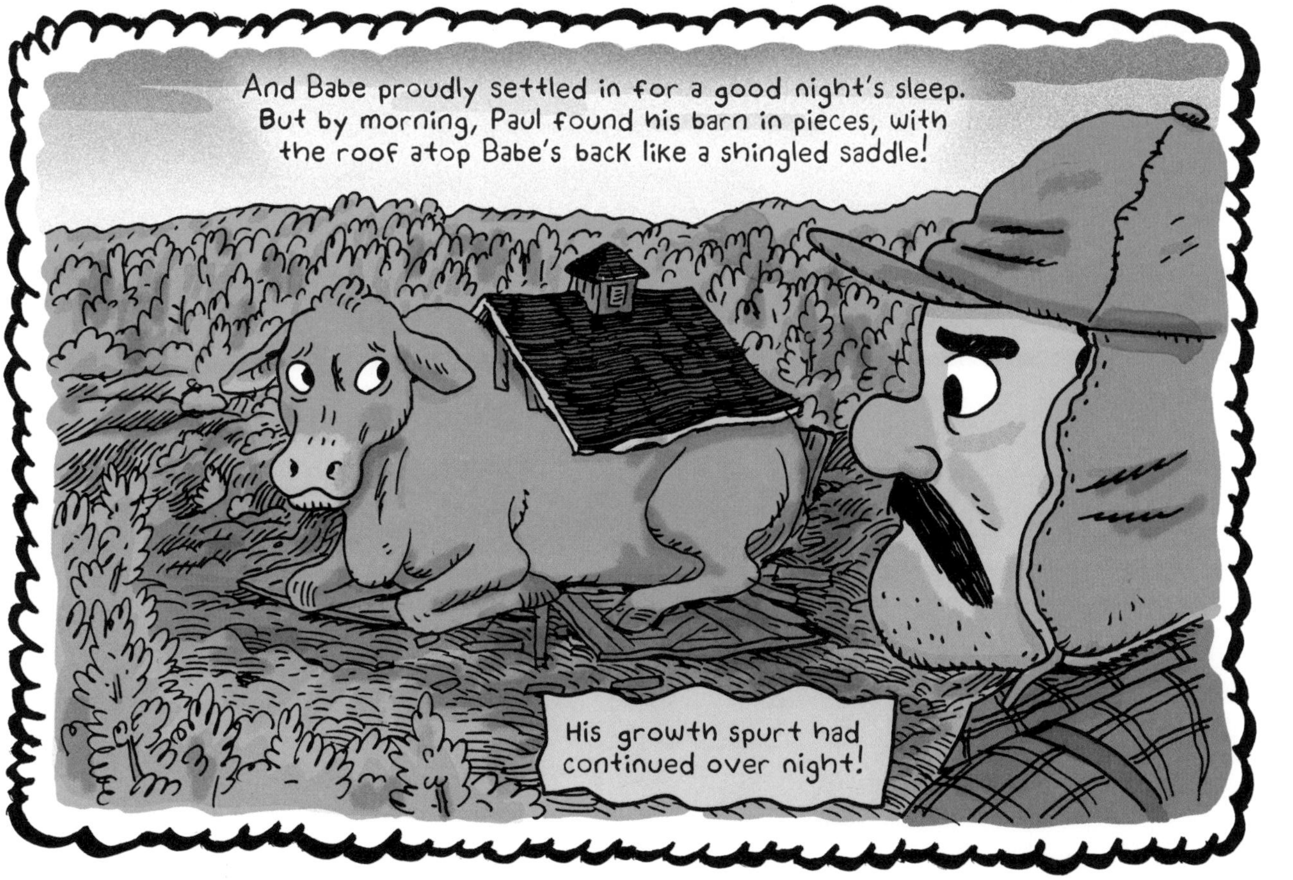
And Babe proudly settled in for a good night's sleep. But by morning, Paul found his barn in pieces, with the roof atop Babe's back like a shingled saddle!
His growth spurt had continued over night!

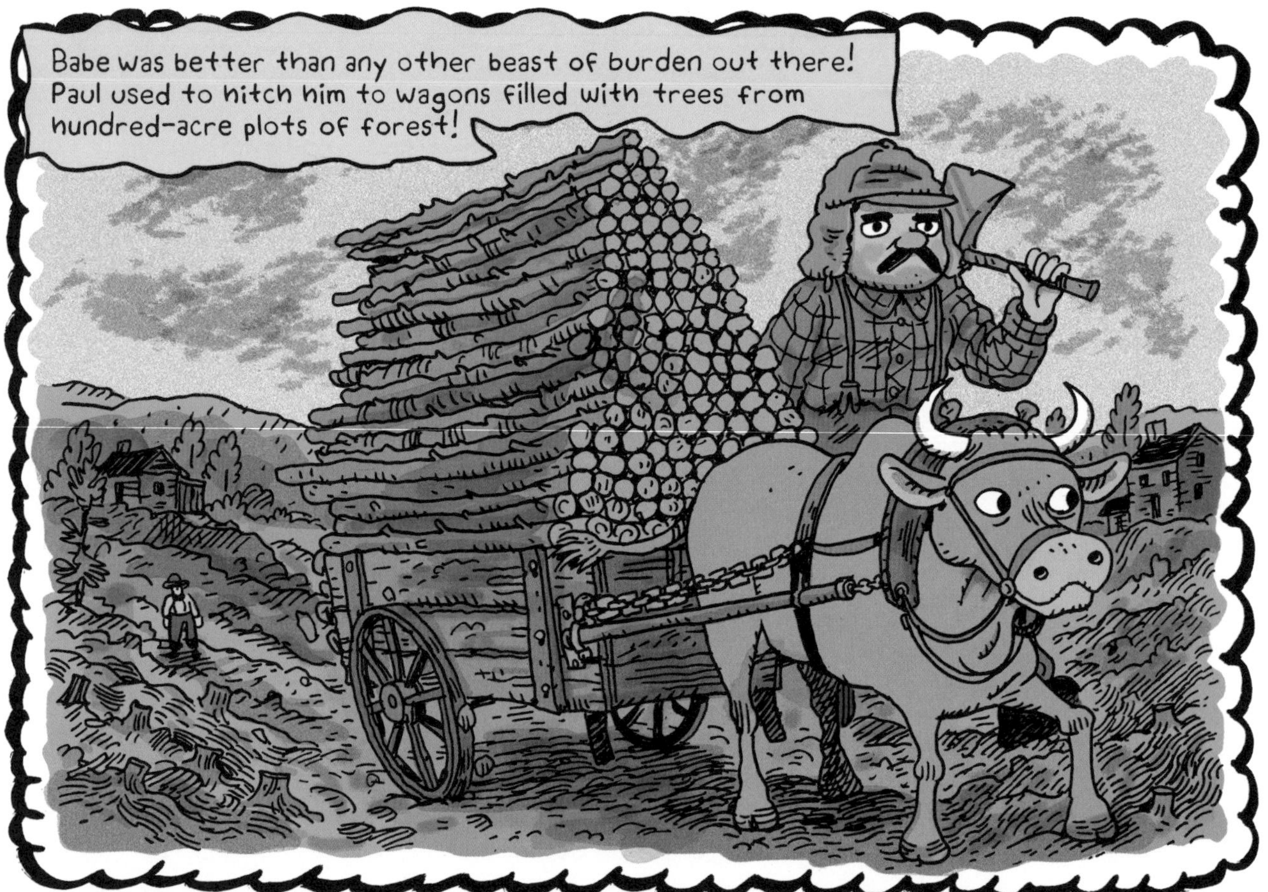
Babe was better than any other beast of burden out there! Paul used to hitch him to wagons filled with trees from hundred-acre plots of forest!

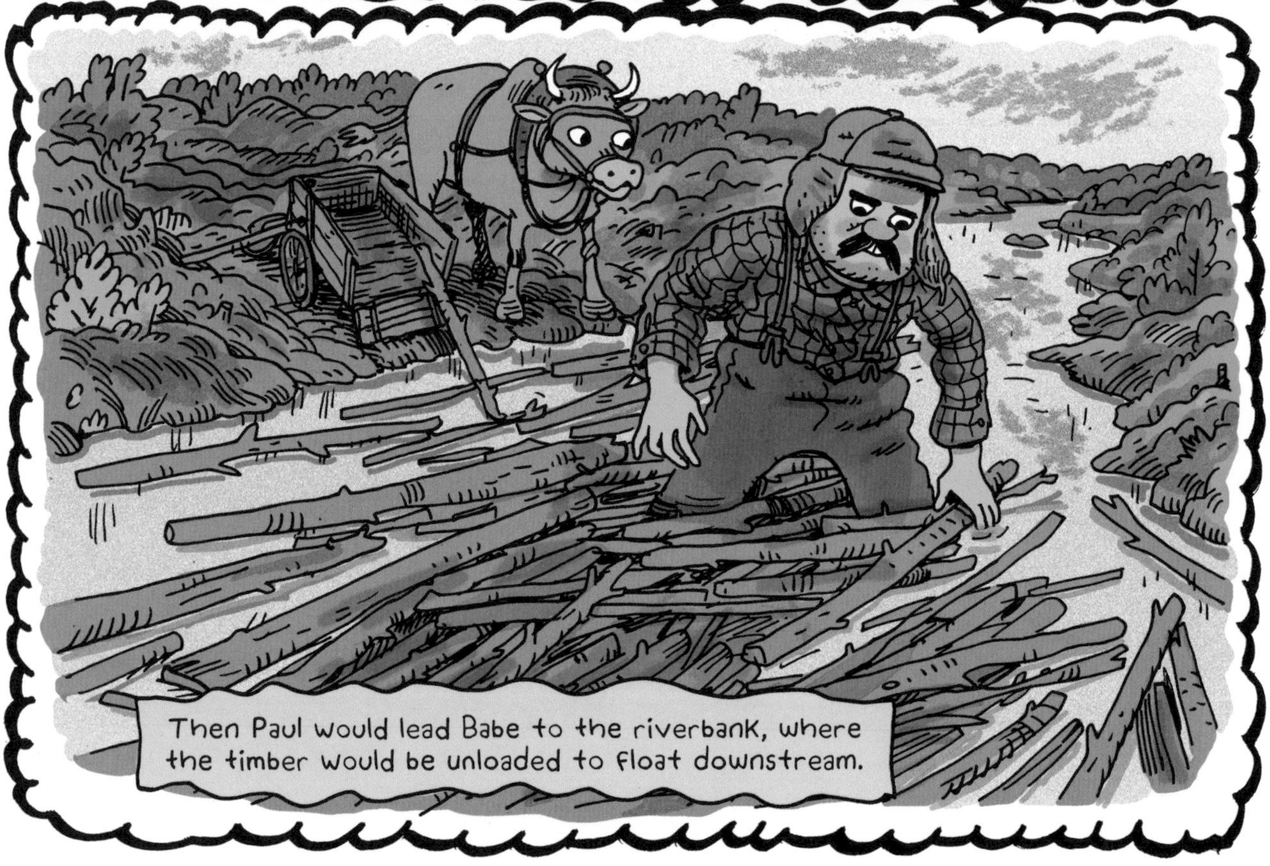
Then Paul would lead Babe to the riverbank, where the timber would be unloaded to float downstream.

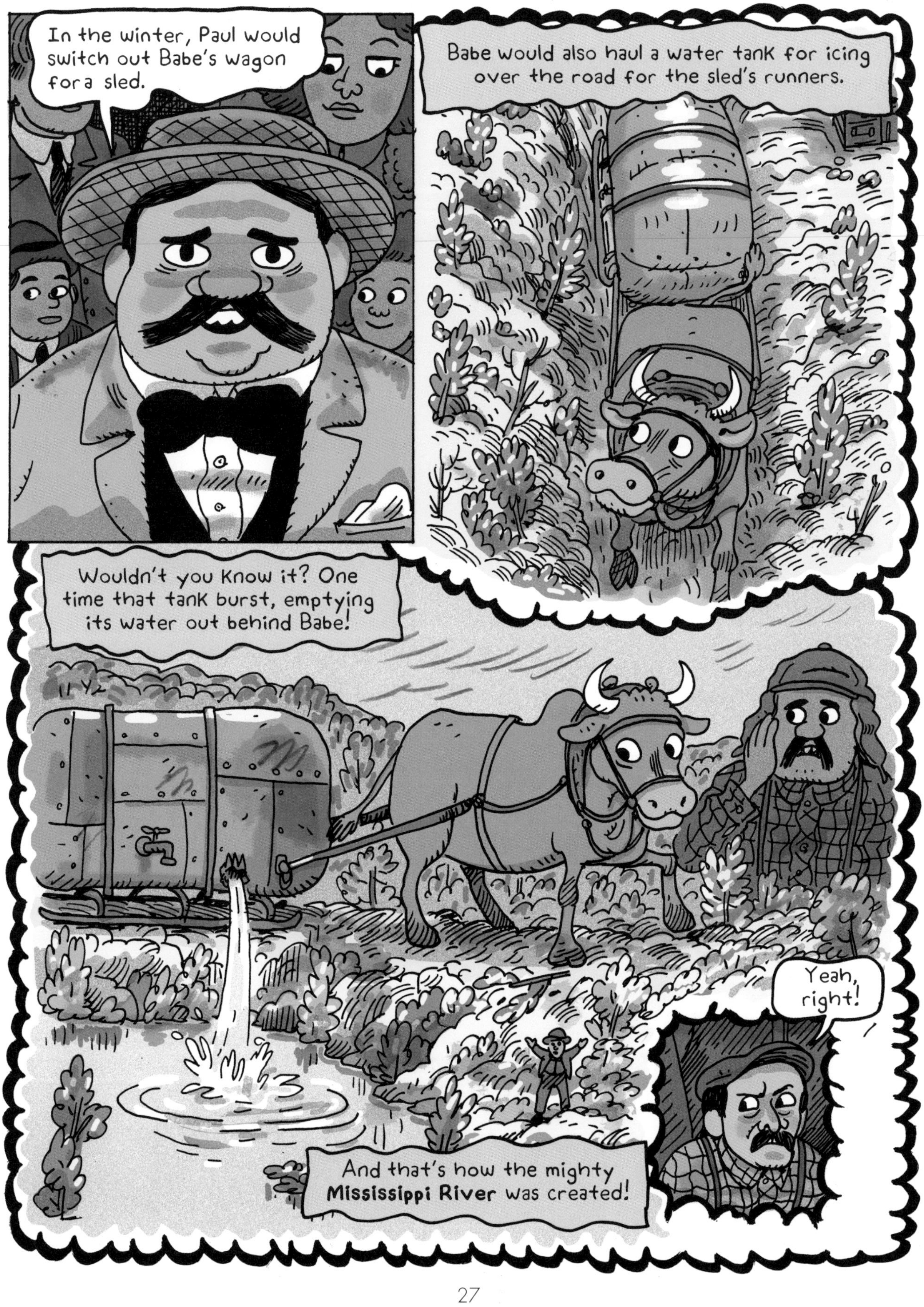
In the winter, Paul would switch out Babe's wagon for a sled.
Babe would also haul a water tank for icing over the road for the sled's runners.
Wouldn't you know it? One time that tank burst, emptying its water out behind Babe!
Yeah, right!
And that's how the mighty **Mississippi River** was created!

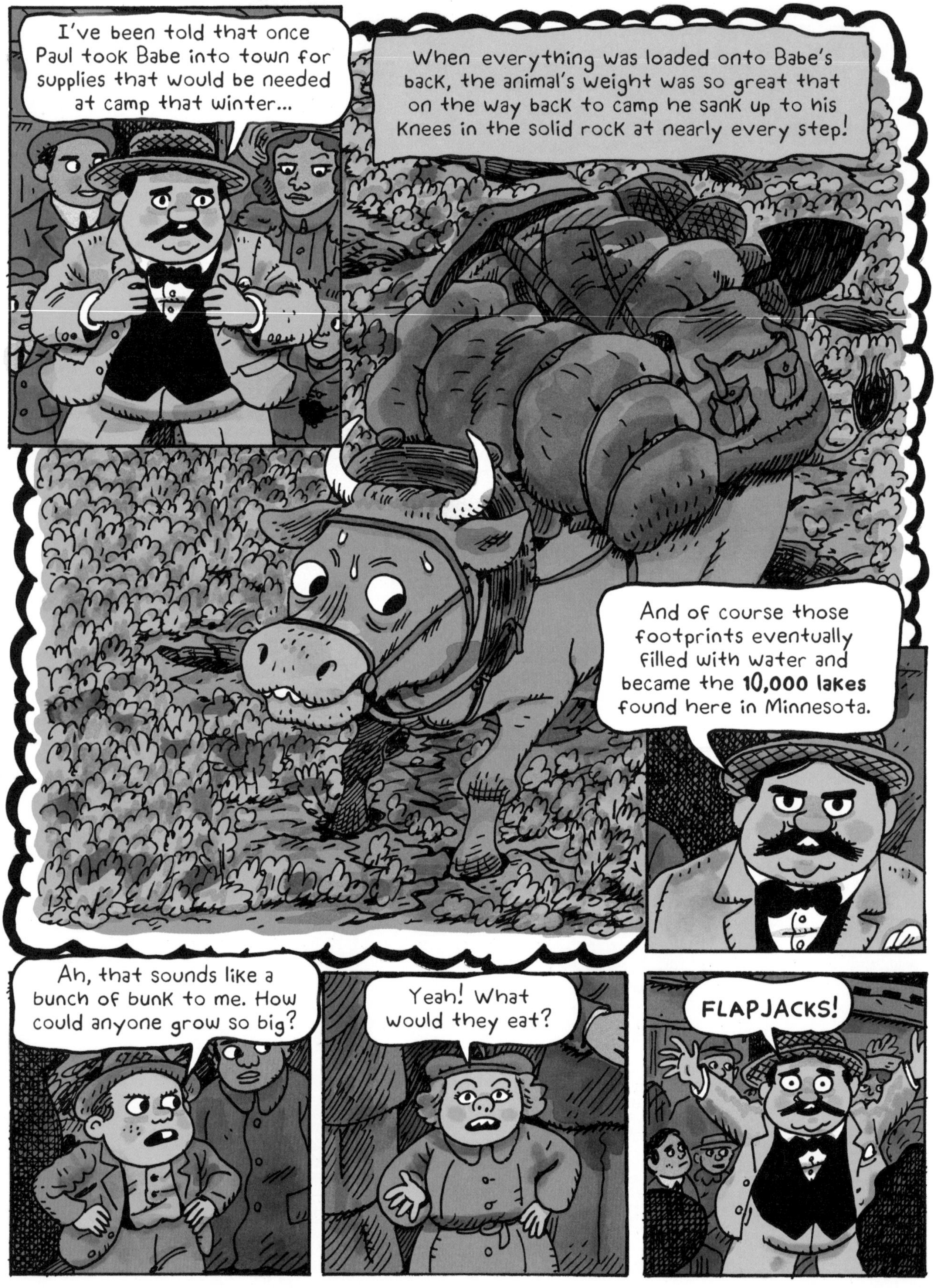

I've been told that once Paul took Babe into town for supplies that would be needed at camp that winter...
When everything was loaded onto Babe's back, the animal's weight was so great that on the way back to camp he sank up to his knees in the solid rock at nearly every step!
And of course those footprints eventually filled with water and became the **10,000 lakes** found here in Minnesota.
Ah, that sounds like a bunch of bunk to me. How could anyone grow so big?
Yeah! What would they eat?
FLAPJACKS!

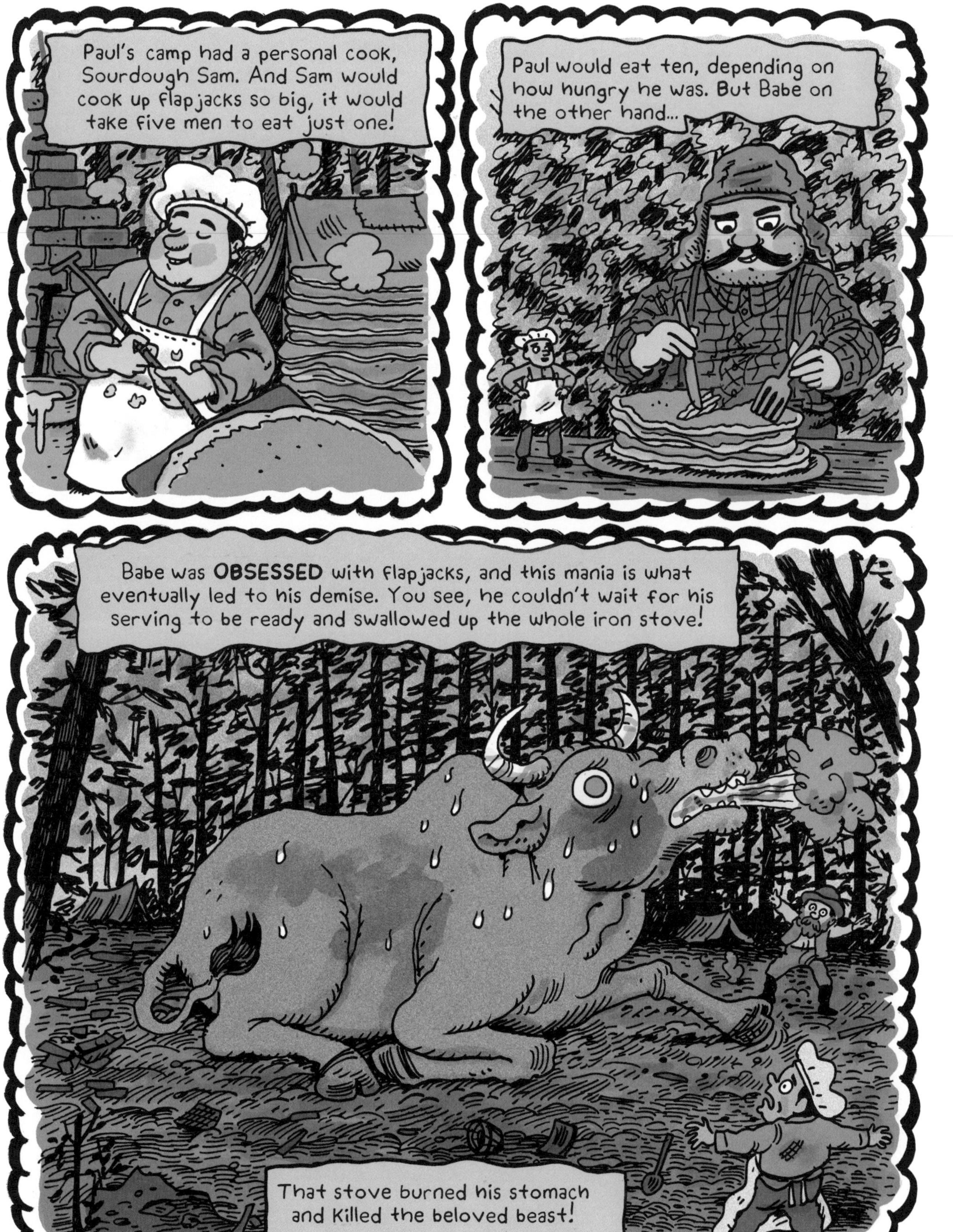
Paul's camp had a personal cook, Sourdough Sam. And Sam would cook up flapjacks so big, it would take five men to eat just one!
Paul would eat ten, depending on how hungry he was. But Babe on the other hand...
Babe was **OBSESSED** with flapjacks, and this mania is what eventually led to his demise. You see, he couldn't wait for his serving to be ready and swallowed up the whole iron stove!
That stove burned his stomach and killed the beloved beast!

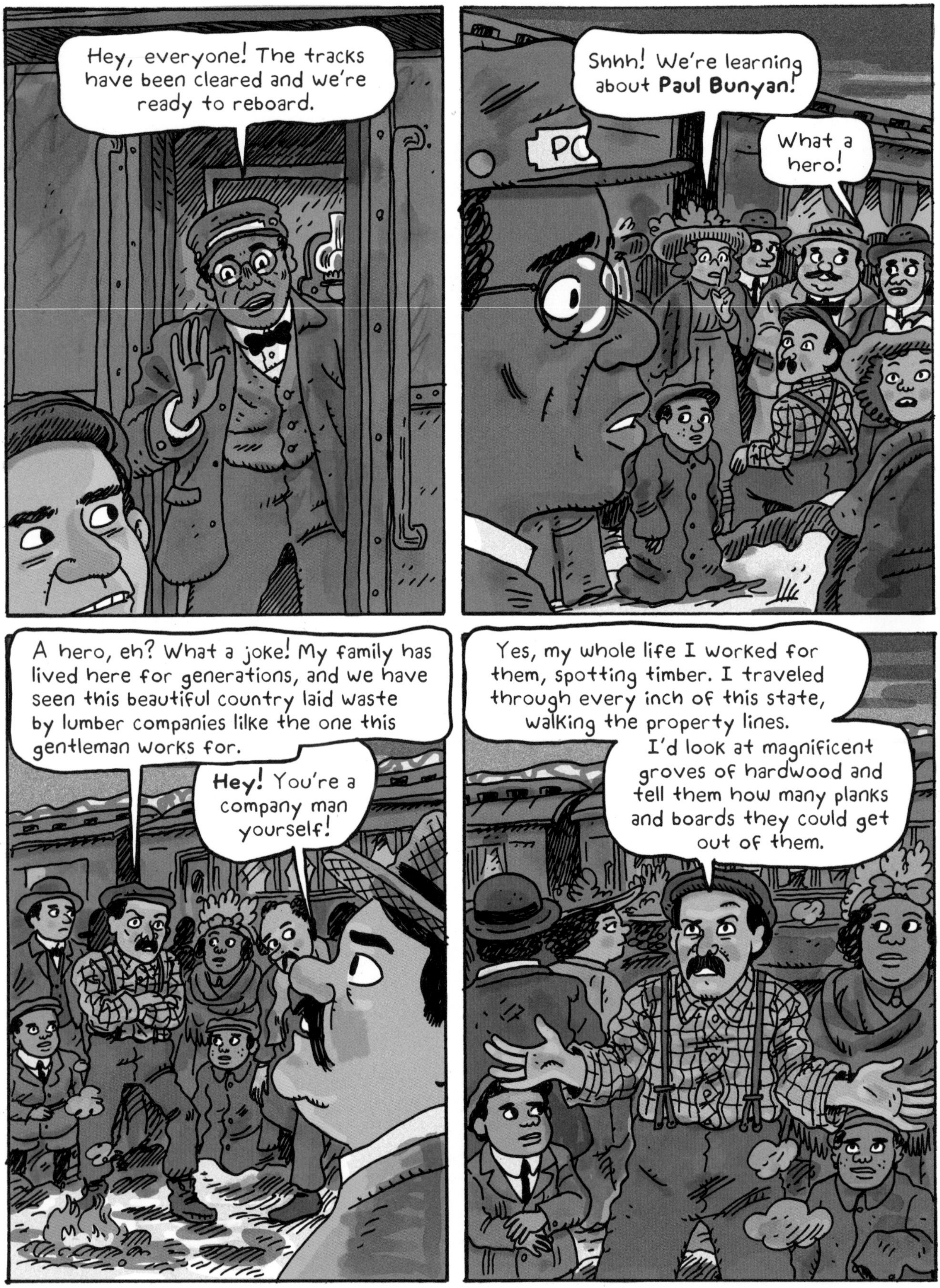
Hey, everyone! The tracks have been cleared and we're ready to reboard.
Shhh! We're learning about **Paul Bunyan**!
What a hero!
A hero, eh? What a joke! My family has lived here for generations, and we have seen this beautiful country laid waste by lumber companies like the one this gentleman works for.
Hey! You're a company man yourself!
Yes, my whole life I worked for them, spotting timber. I traveled through every inch of this state, walking the property lines.
I'd look at magnificent groves of hardwood and tell them how many planks and boards they could get out of them.

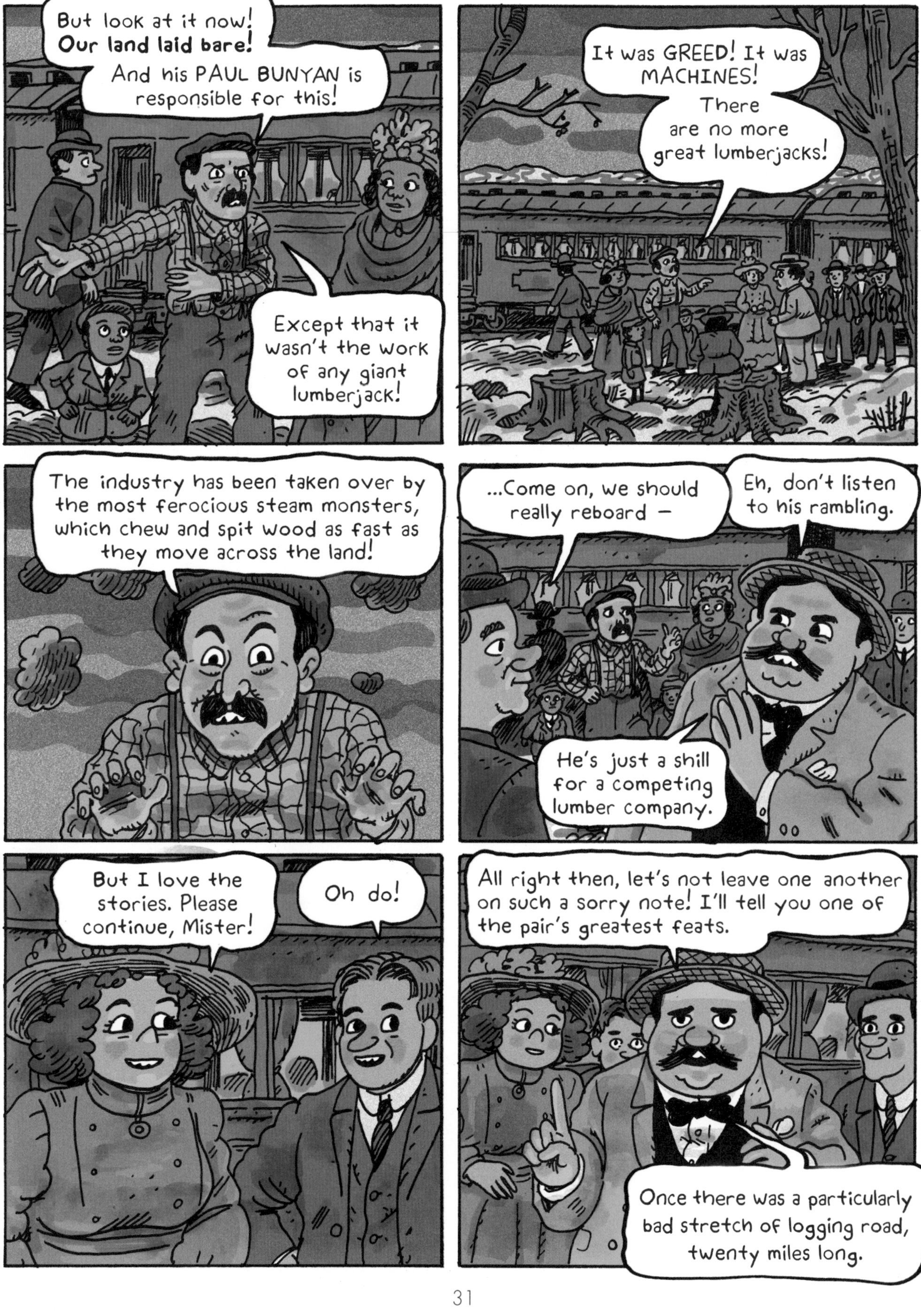
But look at it now! **Our land laid bare!**
And his PAUL BUNYAN is responsible for this!
Except that it wasn't the work of any giant lumberjack!
It was GREED! It was MACHINES!
There are no more great lumberjacks!
The industry has been taken over by the most ferocious steam monsters, which chew and spit wood as fast as they move across the land!
...Come on, we should really reboard —
Eh, don't listen to his rambling.
He's just a shill for a competing lumber company.
But I love the stories. Please continue, Mister!
Oh do!
All right then, let's not leave one another on such a sorry note! I'll tell you one of the pair's greatest feats.
Once there was a particularly bad stretch of logging road, twenty miles long.

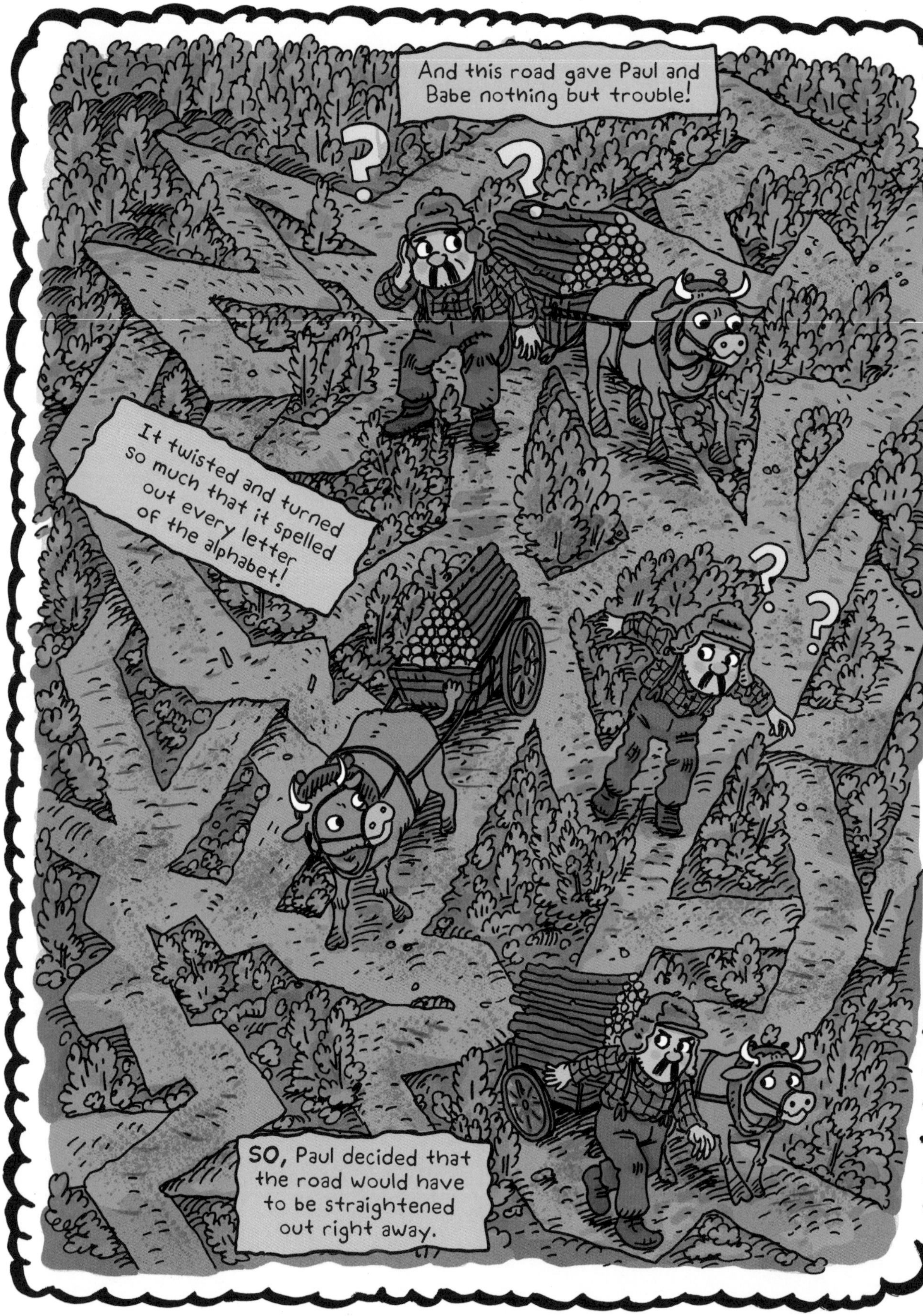
And this road gave Paul and Babe nothing but trouble!
It twisted and turned so much that it spelled out every letter of the alphabet!
SO, Paul decided that the road would have to be straightened out right away.

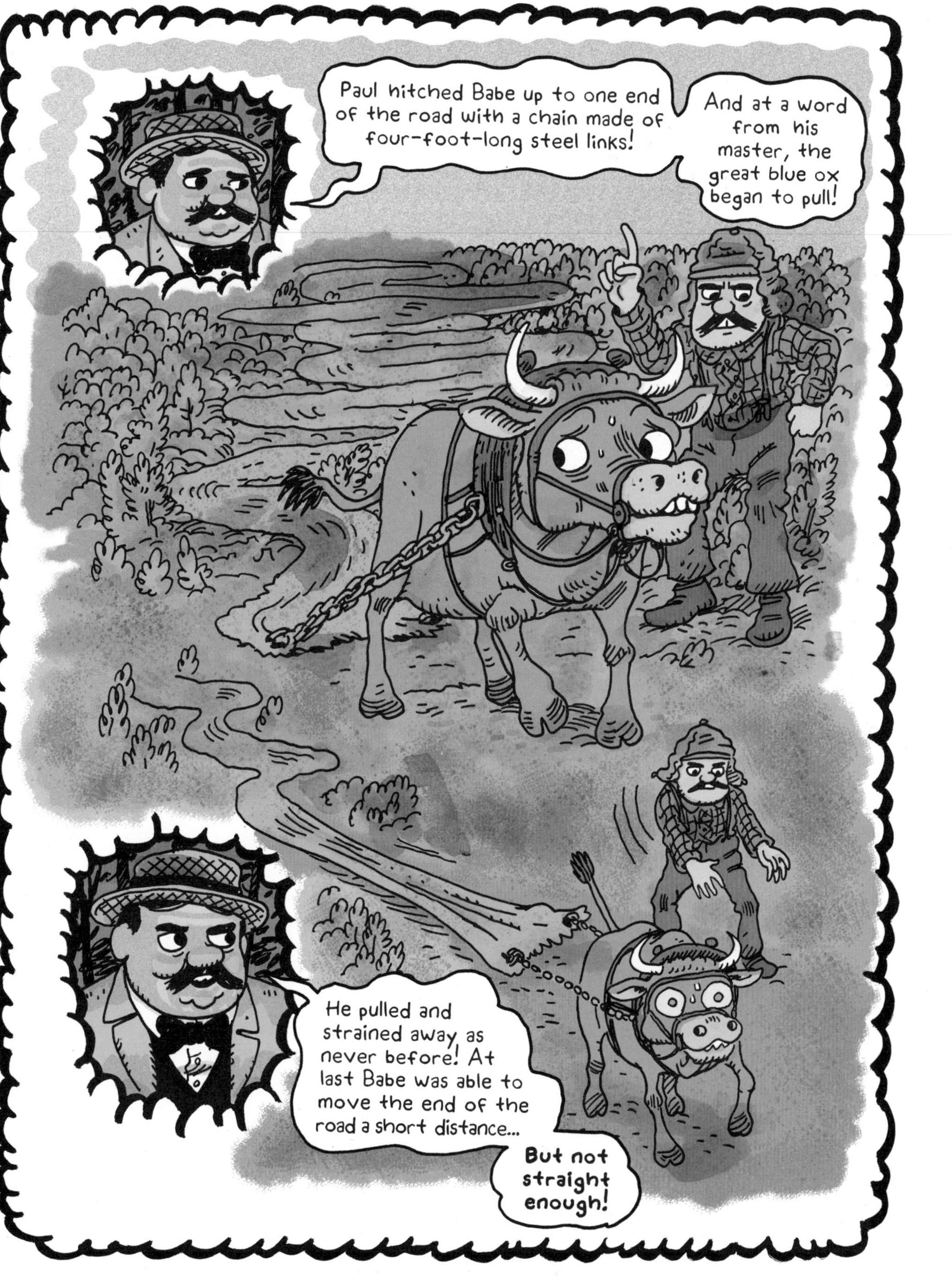
Paul hitched Babe up to one end of the road with a chain made of four-foot-long steel links!
And at a word from his master, the great blue ox began to pull!
He pulled and strained away as never before! At last Babe was able to move the end of the road a short distance...
But not straight enough!

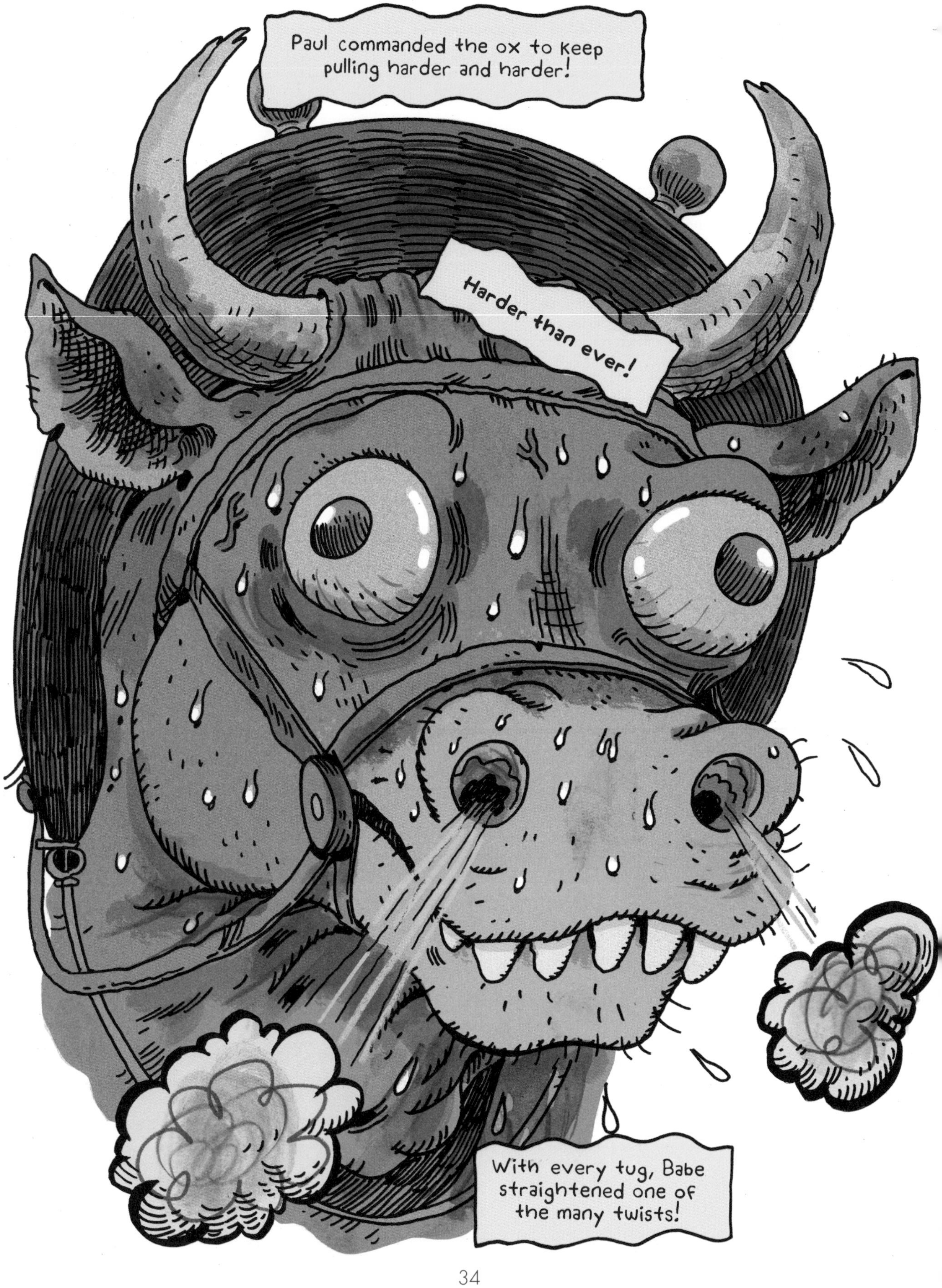
Paul commanded the ox to keep pulling harder and harder!
Harder than ever!
With every tug, Babe straightened one of the many twists!

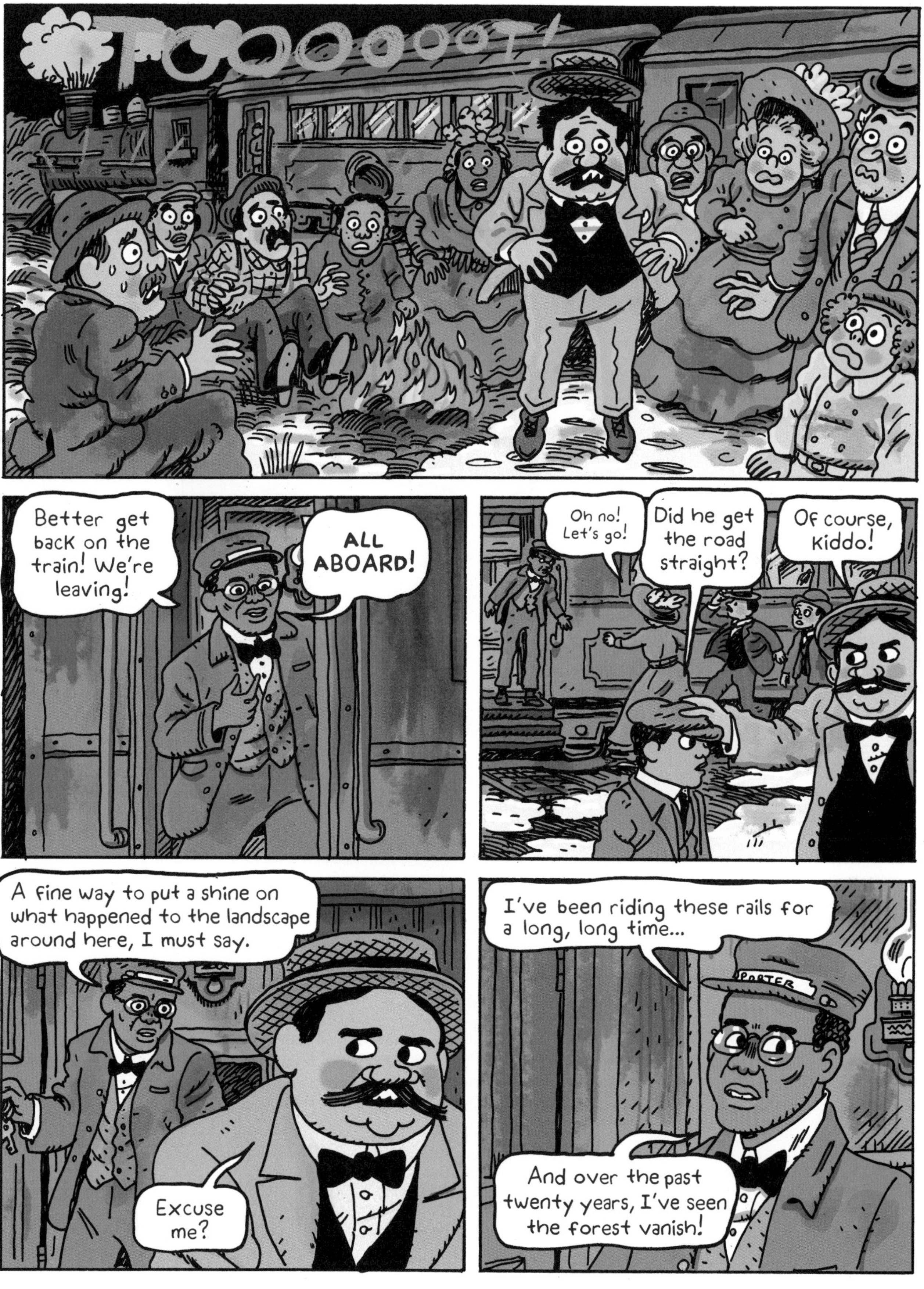
TOOOOOOT!
Better get back on the train! We're leaving!
ALL ABOARD!
Oh no! Let's go!
Did he get the road straight?
Of course, kiddo!
A fine way to put a shine on what happened to the landscape around here, I must say.
Excuse me?
I've been riding these rails for a long, long time...
PORTER
And over the past twenty years, I've seen the forest vanish!

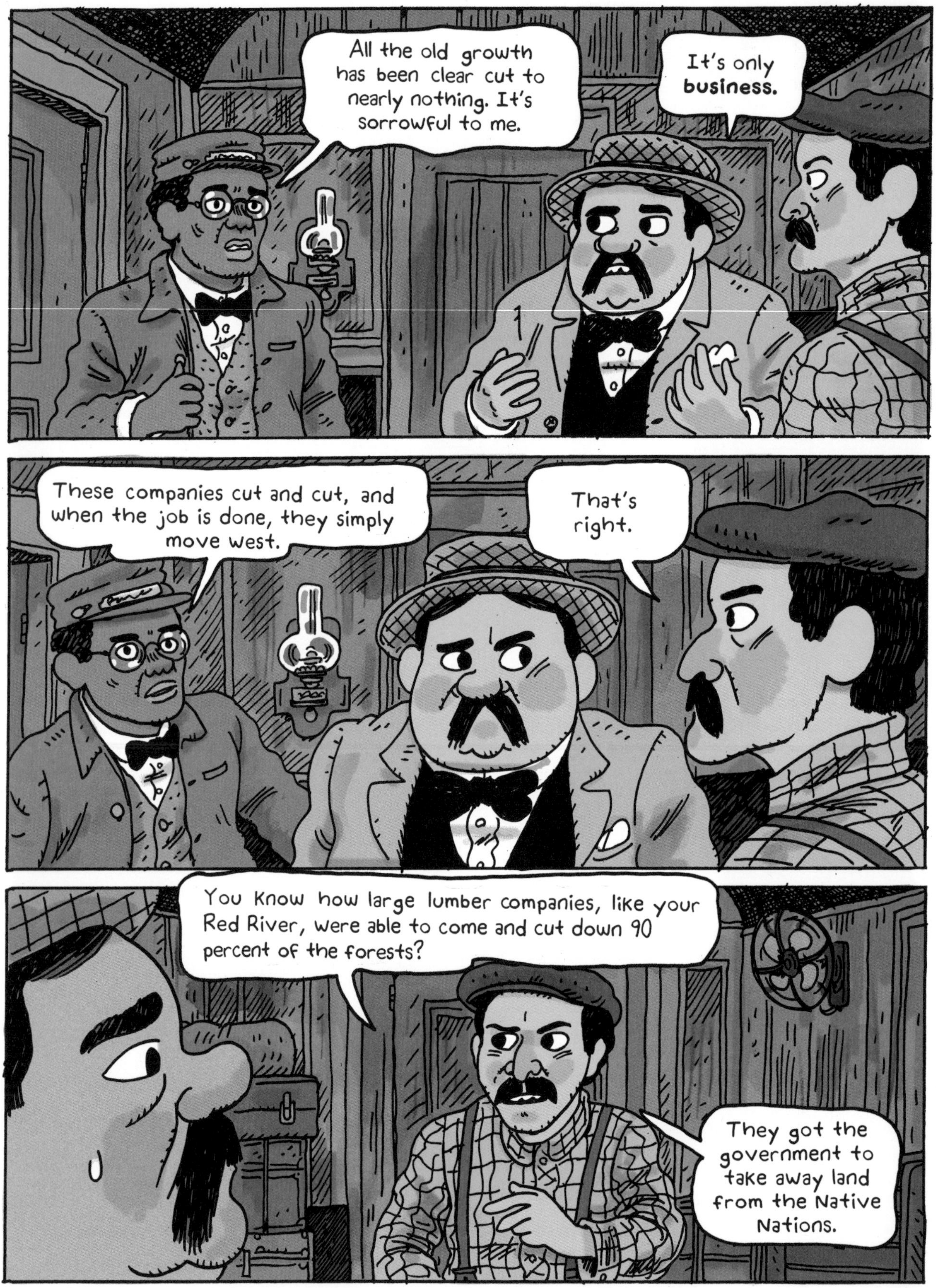
All the old growth has been clear cut to nearly nothing. It's sorrowful to me.
It's only **business.**
These companies cut and cut, and when the job is done, they simply move west.
That's right.
You know how large lumber companies, like your Red River, were able to come and cut down 90 percent of the forests?
They got the government to take away land from the Native Nations.

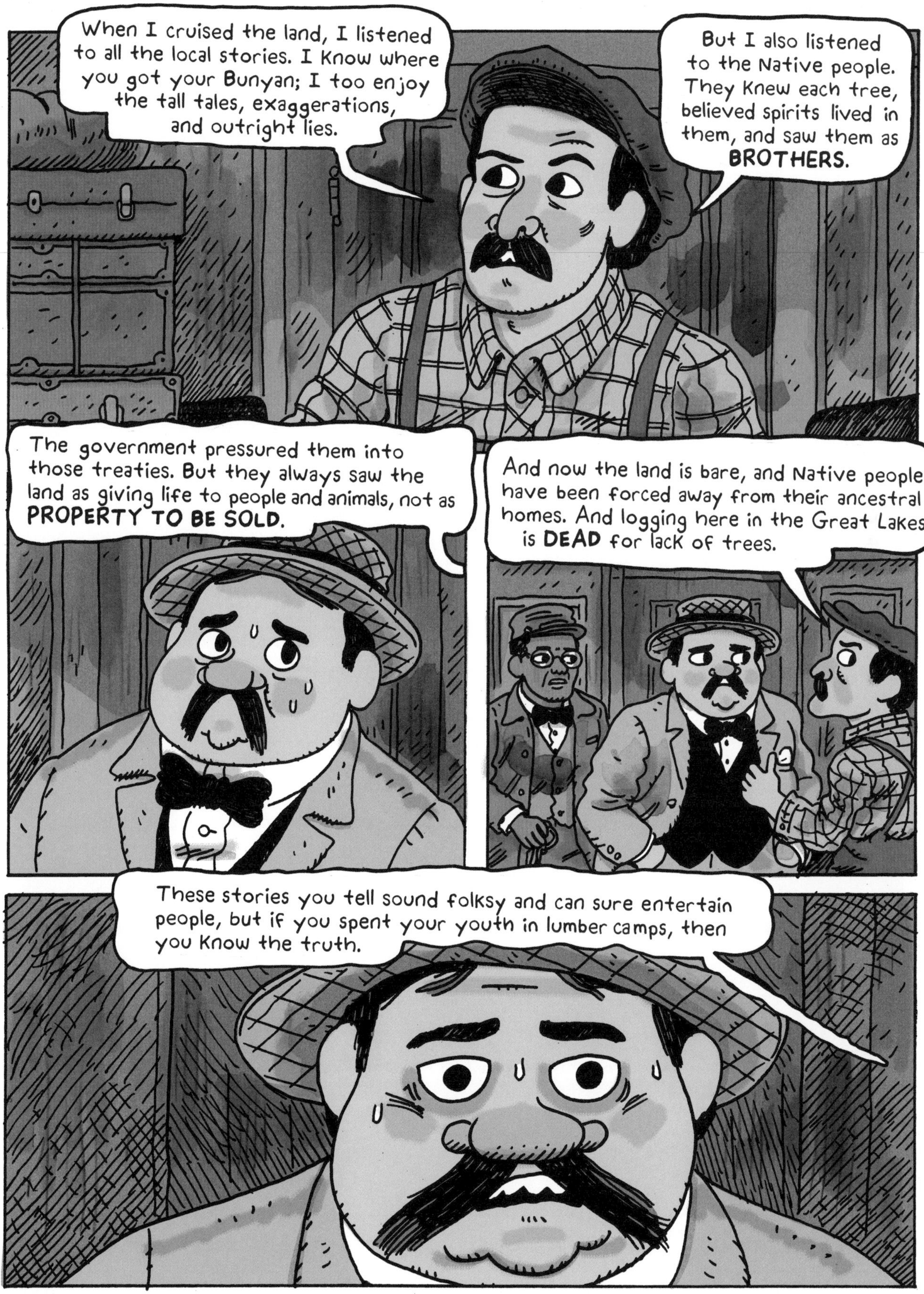
When I cruised the land, I listened to all the local stories. I know where you got your Bunyan; I too enjoy the tall tales, exaggerations, and outright lies.
But I also listened to the Native people. They knew each tree, believed spirits lived in them, and saw them as BROTHERS.
The government pressured them into those treaties. But they always saw the land as giving life to people and animals, not as PROPERTY TO BE SOLD.
And now the land is bare, and Native people have been forced away from their ancestral homes. And logging here in the Great Lakes is DEAD for lack of trees.
These stories you tell sound folksy and can sure entertain people, but if you spent your youth in lumber camps, then you know the truth.

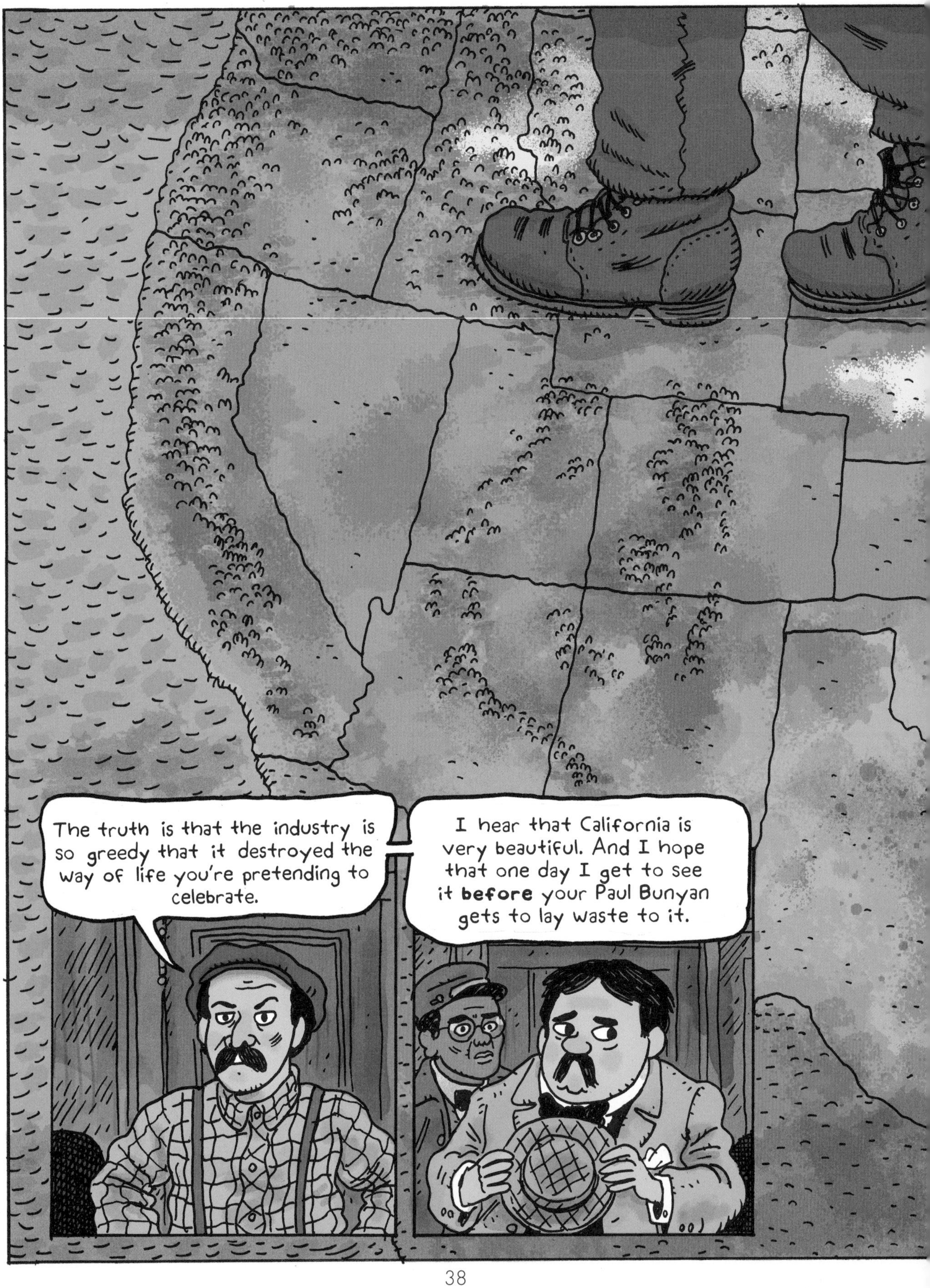
The truth is that the industry is so greedy that it destroyed the way of life you're pretending to celebrate.
I hear that California is very beautiful. And I hope that one day I get to see it **before** your Paul Bunyan gets to lay waste to it.

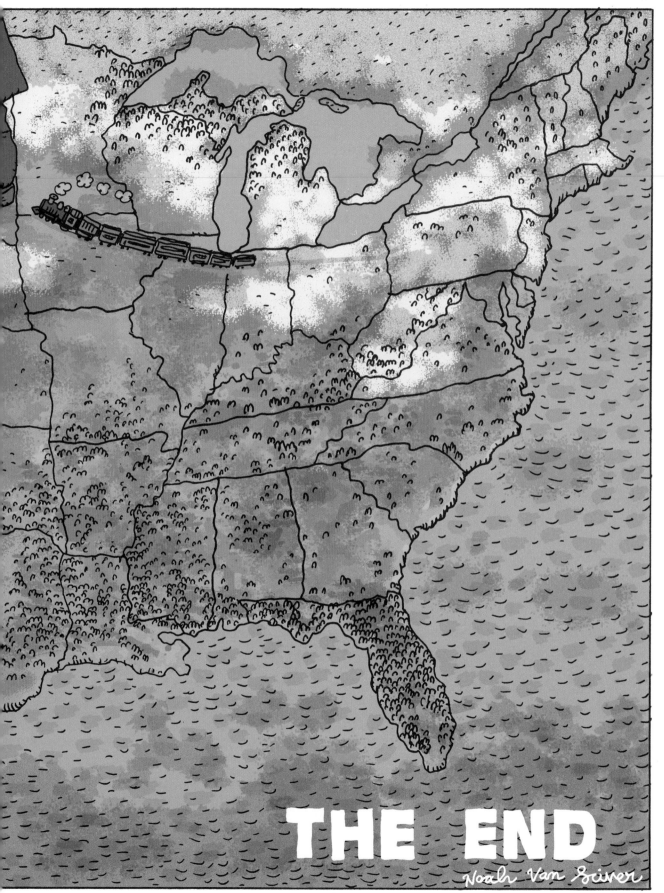

THE END

Noah Van Sciver

THE INVENTION OF AN AMERICAN LEGEND

by Dr. Deondre Smiles
LEECH LAKE BAND OF OJIBWE

When I was growing up as a young Ojibwe child in Minnesota, Paul Bunyan loomed very large in my life, as he does in the lives of many children in the state—quite literally sometimes. Whenever my mother took me up to our tribe's reservation in northern Minnesota, we'd often stop in the nearby town of Bemidji for shopping, local food, or anything that we couldn't find in the small town where our extended family lived. And there stood a giant statue of Paul Bunyan and his faithful companion, Babe the Blue Ox—they're still there to the present day. I also read about Bunyan in a colorful storybook that I got from a trading post, right across the street from the statue. It wasn't until I was much older and was working toward my graduate degrees that I realized that the story of Paul Bunyan, exciting as it was, hid the harmful things that colonization has done to Indigenous peoples and environments in the United States. When I first tried to teach this to my students, many of them were shocked and in disbelief—Paul Bunyan is only a story, they'd tell me. There was nothing sinister or harmful about these tales, they'd argue. I knew I had to tell them more about what the landscape was like before the "era" of Paul Bunyan. Prior to colonization by European settlers, about half of what we now know as the United States was covered by one billion (a thousand million) acres of forests, including the birch, aspen, and white spruce trees that were common in the Great Lakes region. We refer to these woods, growing undisturbed by humans, as "old-growth," "native," or "virgin" forests.

When Europeans arrived, they were appalled by the harsh winters and humid summers they experienced in North America. Some thought cutting down trees would allow for more air and

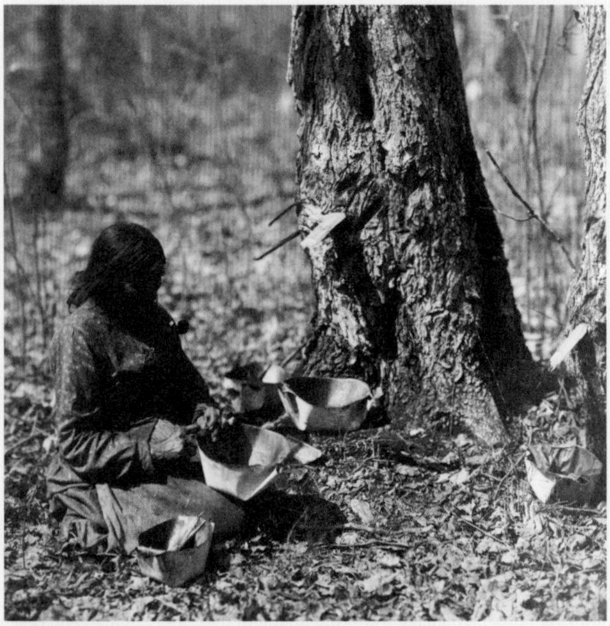

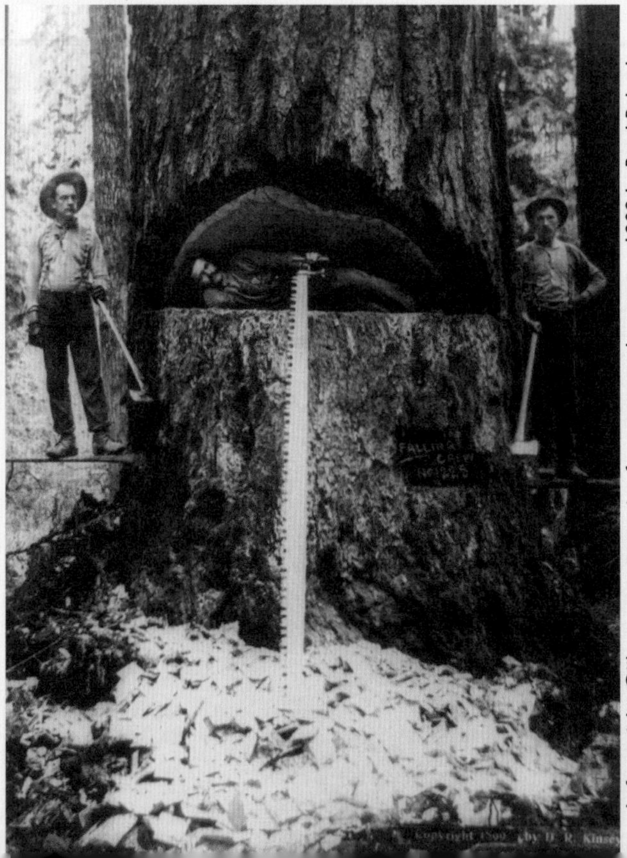

Left: *An Ojibwe woman taps a maple tree for its sap to make maple syrup. The sap is later boiled over an outdoor fire.* Right: *Loggers in 1899 pose with an enormous tree they are cutting down. It takes hundreds of years for a tree to reach such a size. Mature trees are also one of nature's most effective forms of carbon storage.*

Left to right: Ojibwe woman tapping for sugar maple syrup, c. *1908 by Reed Roland.* • Falling Crew, c. *1899 © D R Kinsey. Both images courtesy: Library of Congress.*

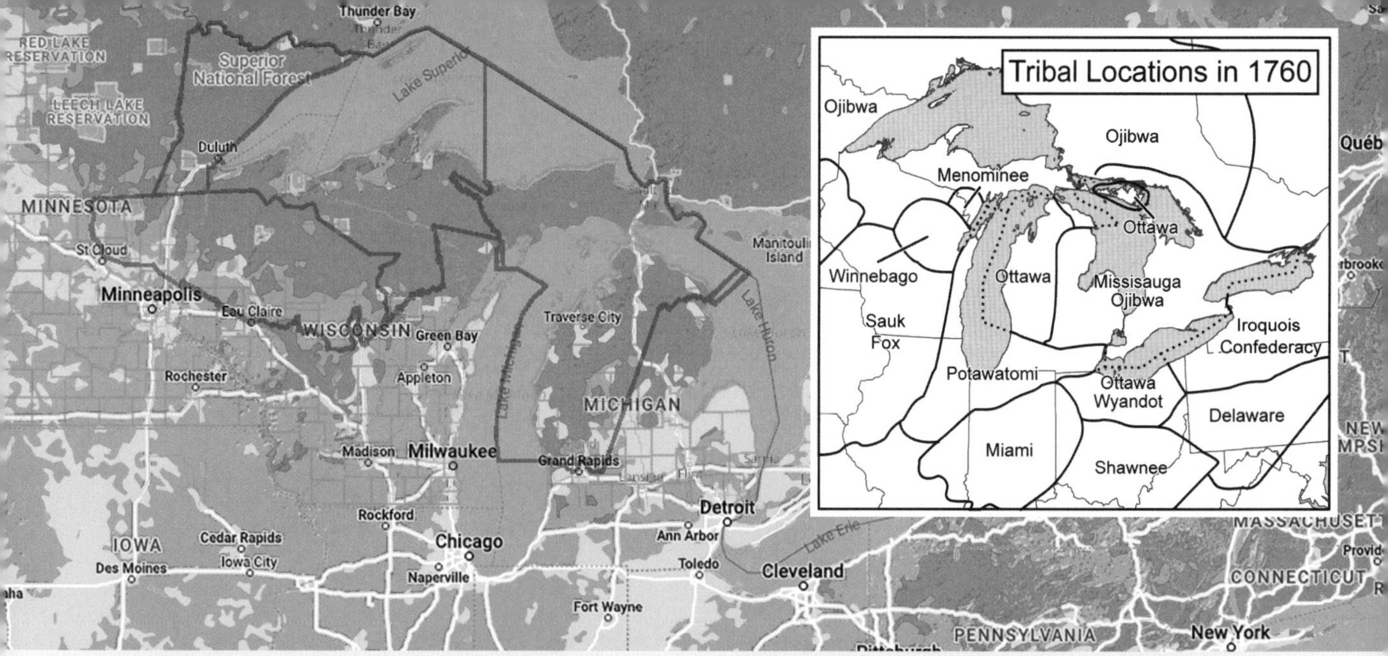
Tribal Locations in 1760
Ojibwa
Ojibwa
Menominee
Ottawa
Winnebago
Ottawa
Missisauga
Ojibwa
Sauk
Fox
Iroquois
Confederacy
Potawatomi
Ottawa
Wyandot
Delaware
Miami
Shawnee
Thunder Bay
RED LAKE RESERVATION
Superior National Forest
LEECH LAKE RESERVATION
Lake Superior
Duluth
MINNESOTA
St Cloud
Minneapolis
Eau Claire
WISCONSIN
Green Bay
Manitoulin Island
Traverse City
Lake Huron
Lake Michigan
Rochester
Appleton
MICHIGAN
Madison
Milwaukee
Grand Rapids
Rockford
Detroit
IOWA
Cedar Rapids
Iowa City
Des Moines
Chicago
Ann Arbor
Lake Erie
Toledo
Naperville
Cleveland
Fort Wayne
PENNSYLVANIA
New York
MASSACHUSETTS
CONNECTICUT

CEDED TERRITORIES (outlined in red): *From 1836 to 1854, large pieces of land were transferred from tribal ownership to settler/American ownership via treaties or agreements. Under pressure, tribes agreed to open territories for settlement and relocate elsewhere, often onto reservations set aside for them by the United States government. Although these treaties were supposed to protect Native rights to hunt, fish, and gather within the "ceded territories," the Federal and state governments rarely respected these rights, leading to long-standing struggles by Native tribes to protect and assert them.*

sunlight, and many advocated for changing the climate by clear-cutting the dense forests. In a 1763 letter, Benjamin Franklin wrote, "Cleared land absorbs more heat and melts snow quicker," which was an avowed goal. By the early 1800s, settlers were happy to see that snowfall in New England was less than half of what it had been fifty years earlier. And by the 1850s, as the demand for wood products skyrocketed (before it was replaced by oil, wood was the primary source of energy, and logs were needed for construction and railroad ties), no one objected when millions of acres of trees were cut down by logging companies, including Minnesota's Red River Lumber Company. Today, it's estimated that less than 10 percent of old-growth forests remain in the lower 48 states, and catastrophic climate change is well underway.

But the damage wasn't limited to environments. Indigenous peoples as well were harmed by this assault on their land and resources. In the 19th century, with the relentless push westward of settlers and logging companies, they urged the Federal government to intervene on their behalf. Access to the indigenous forests was gained through violence by settlers and the US military and by signing treaties with Indigenous Nations. These treaties were often signed under unfair or inequitable conditions, and Indigenous Nations were forced to move away from lands they had lived on for generations. Huge amounts of land were seized in exchange for modest monetary payments and continued rights to hunting, fishing, and gathering. This also led to the creation of "reservations," parcels of land for Indigenous Nations to live on. The dispossession did not cease there—some tribes, such as mine, own only a small percentage of the lands on their reservations.

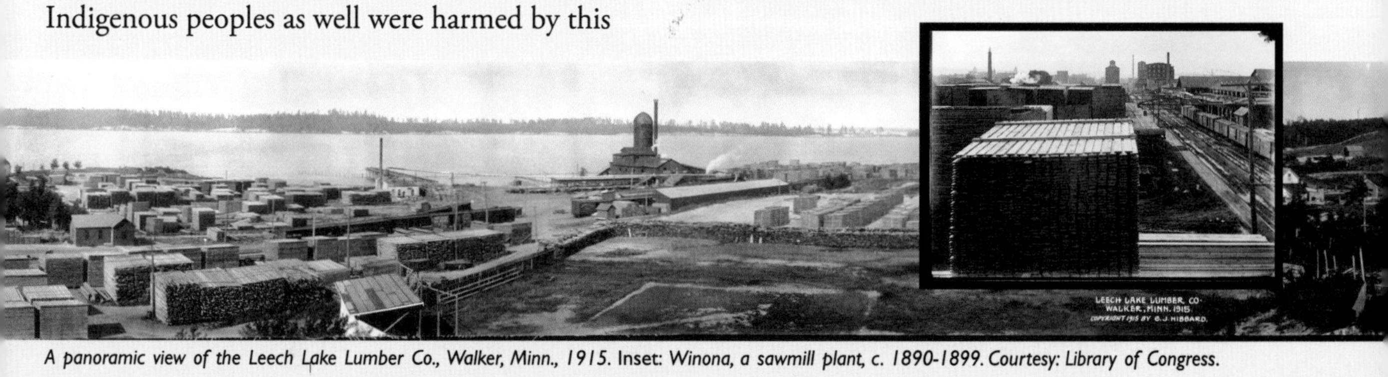
LEECH LAKE LUMBER CO.
WALKER, MINN. 1915

A panoramic view of the Leech Lake Lumber Co., Walker, Minn., 1915. Inset: *Winona, a sawmill plant, c. 1890-1899. Courtesy: Library of Congress.*

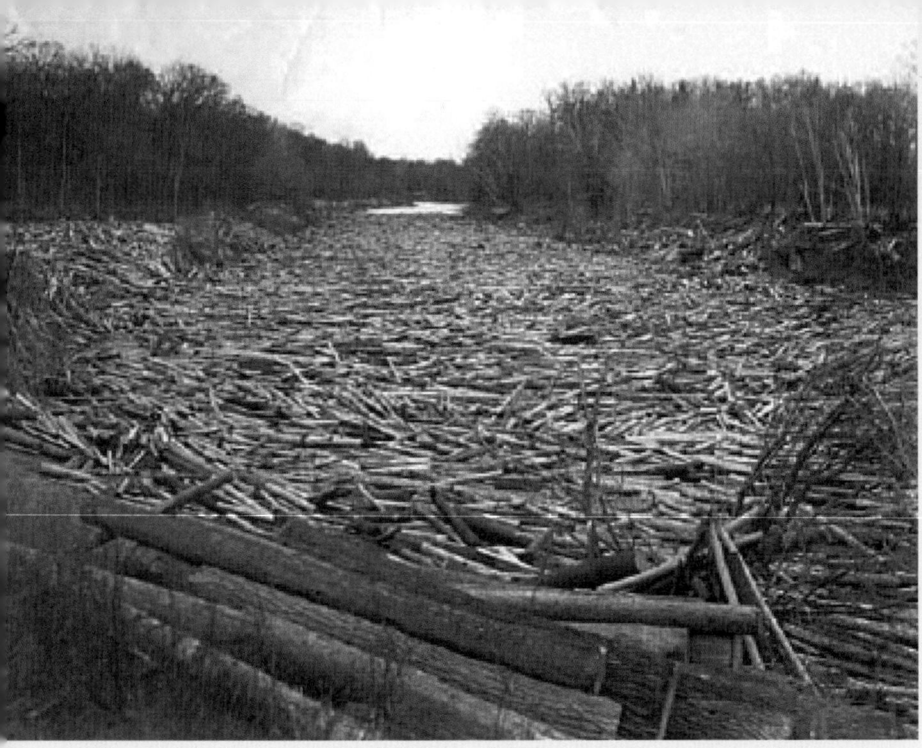

Tail end of a log jam on the Little Fork River, *c. 1935. Courtesy: Minnesota Historical Society.*

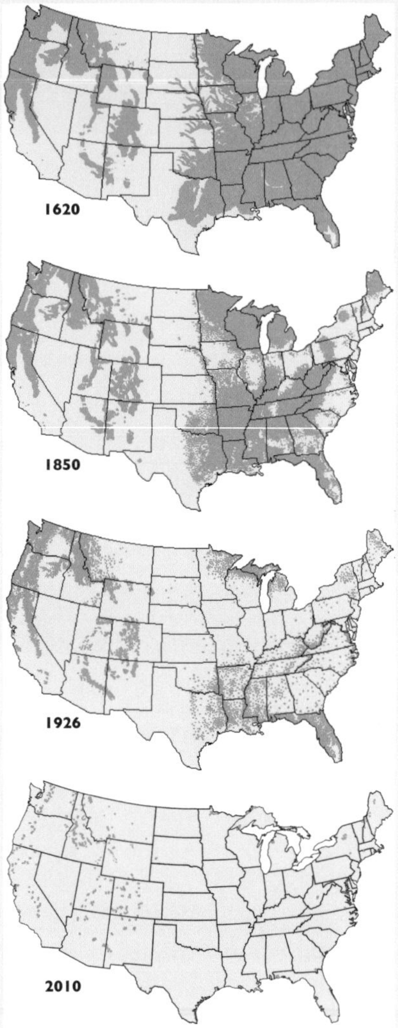
1620
1850
1926
2010

Area of old growth forest in the continental United States: 1620 vs 1850 vs 1926 vs present day.

1620, 1850, and 1926 maps, c. 1926. Courtesy: United States Forestry Service. 2010 map © George Draffan.

I teach my students this history and tie it to our present-day ways for understanding our relationship to the land. In Minnesota, which tries to present itself as an environmentally friendly state, we must not erase Indigenous presences and histories from the land. It is important to acknowledge the history of domestic deforestation before we condemn the same practices elsewhere. My students often ask what they can do. The good news is that it's easy: you can help by supporting the many local efforts already underway. You can help Indigenous efforts to draw awareness to our histories. You can support industries and businesses that practice sustainable forms of production, including resource exploitation. The Leech Lake Tribal College, in Cass Lake, Minnesota, for example, is training graduates to work on an array of community solar gardens. With your support, we can push back together and help Indigenous Nations strive for a more just future for all.

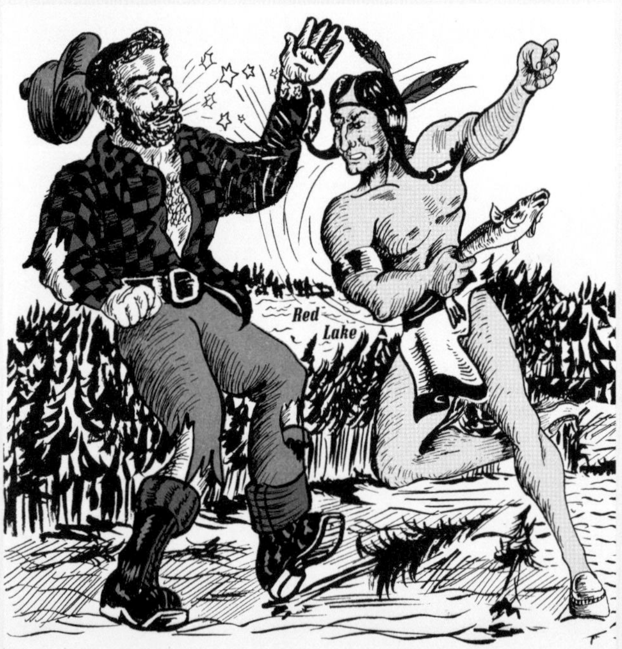
Red
Lake

Ojibwe postcard featuring Na-na-bu-shu's Fight with Paul Bunyan
© 1994 Red Lake Band of Chippewa. Courtesy: Minnesota Historical Society.

In Ojibwe tales, Nanabozho, also known as Nanabush, is a half spirit/half human who has the powers of a spirit and the virtues and flaws of a human being. In a tale, Nanabozho fights Paul Bunyan to make him stop the devastation he's wrought, culminating in Nanabozho's swinging a Red Lake walleye fish at the lumberjack.

TREE-DWELLING LITTLE PEOPLE

Text and art
by Marlena Myles

SPIRIT LAKE DAKOTA

When I visited the Mall of America in Bloomington, Minnesota, I was shocked to see that the mural of Minnesota—which prominently featured Paul Bunyan (and Prince)—made no mention of my people or of any other Indigenous people. It's high time that we looked into Bunyan's origins and acknowledged those who actually were living on that land. The forests of northern Minnesota are the traditional homelands of the Mdewakanton Dakota, one of the four Santee Sioux bands of the Dakota, of which I'm a member. The Ojibwe people, an Algonquin-speaking tribe, also came to the Great Lakes region and, by the 1800s, were occupying lands in Canada and in Michigan, Minnesota, North Dakota, Illinois, Indiana, and Ohio. The relentless push of the European settlers forcibly removed the Dakota and the Ojibwe from their lands and onto reservations. We may be from different tribes, but culturally, we are all woodland people who lived on the edges of lakes, rivers, and forests and thrived on hunting, fishing, and some farming.

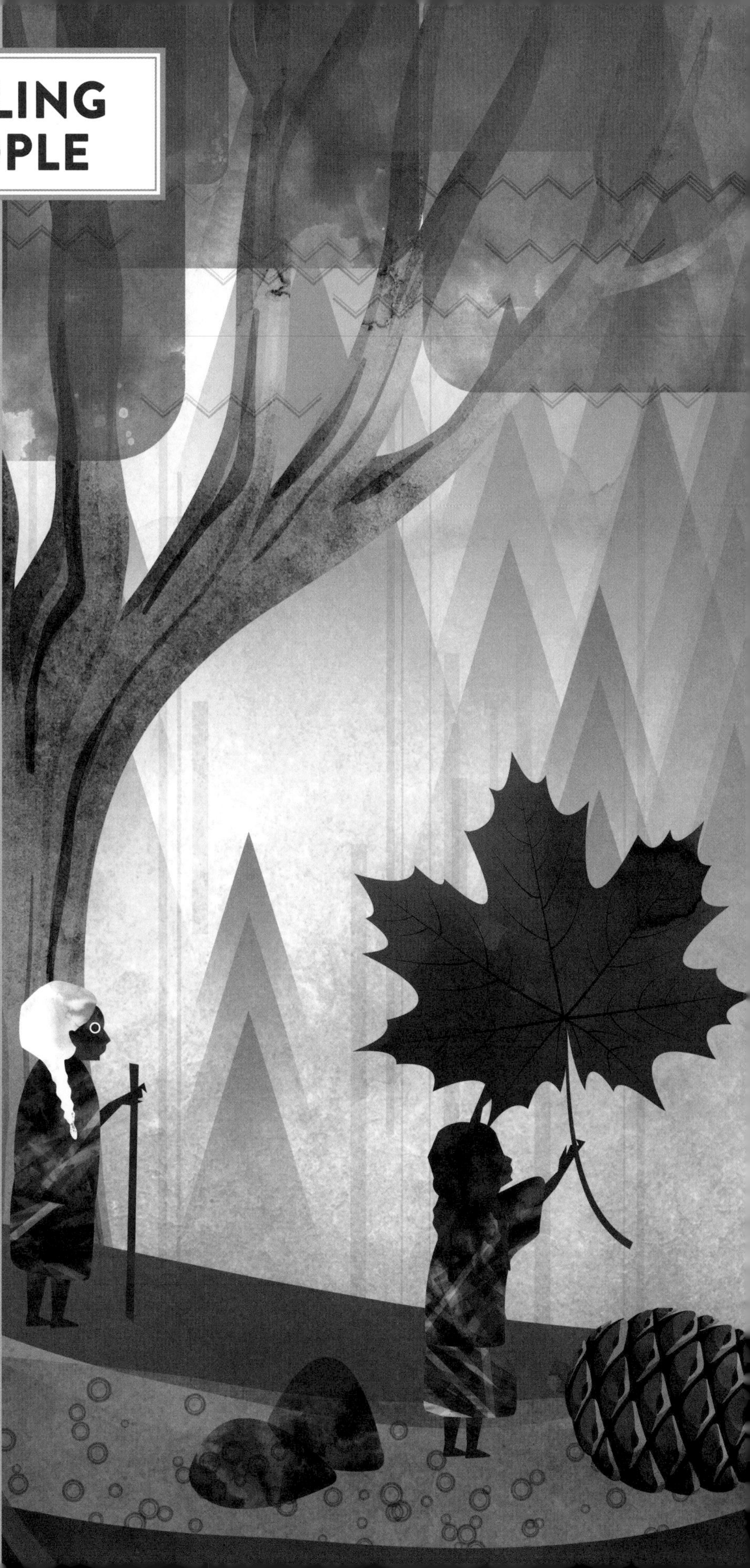

The forests gave rise to many Indigenous stories about wood spirits. Even though these spirits have varying names in different Indigenous languages, almost all tribes have similar stories about Little People. Comparable in size and temperament to what Europeans call fairies or elves, the Little People are often described as living in hollow trees—some say they originate in the bark. On occasion, they use their magical powers to perform such duties as curing illness, seeing into the future, finding missing things, and helping hunters spot game. They also fight thunder beings and have their own weapons to use against other spirits and people. Solitary hunters are led astray, only to find themselves chased, tormented, or set upon by Little People—leading the storyteller to point out that they should have stayed closer to their friends. At other times, when a Little Person turns into an owl and leads a frightened hunter home, the storyteller might use this to show why humility and respect for the wisdom of animals can reward us in a time of need. In a Dakota story, the Chanotidan (or "Little Dwellers of the Woods") attack loggers. Europeans often translated this name as "Little Devils," but the Dakota never forgot that, even if Little People occasionally cause harm, they also give people the gifts of healing and prophecy. The wood spirits can be mischief-makers or healers, but it depends on how you treat them.

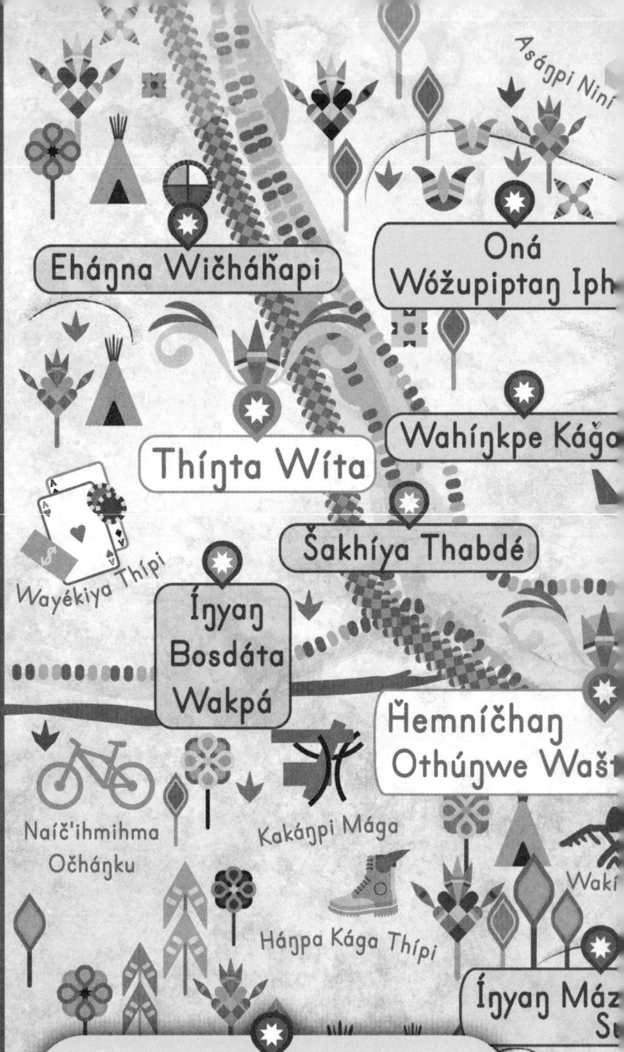
Eháŋna Wičháȟapi
Thíŋta Wíta
Šakhíya Thabdé
Wayékiya Thípi
Íŋyaŋ Bosdáta Wakpá
Naíč'ihmihma Očháŋku
Kakáŋpi Máǧa
Háŋpa Káǧa Thípi

MAP OF Prairie Island • Red Wing • Winona

We are on Dakota homelands

Oral traditions state that Hemníčhaŋ (Barn Bluff), the sacred mountain in Red Wing, was once much larger. Two Dakota villages fought over it. As a compromise, the Great Spirit divided it and moved a portion downriver to Wabasha's Hat in Winona. Another piece of it ended up at Trempealeau Mountain, an island in the Mississipi.

Rivers, Lakes & Other Bodies of Water

Wakpá Tháŋka (Mississippi River)
Šakhíya Thabdé (Sturgeon Lake)
Íŋyaŋ Bosdáta Wakpá (Cannon River)
Tháŋka Bdé (Lake Pepin)
Mniówe (Springs @ Wabasha)
Wazí Ožú Wakpá (Zumbro River)
Mniská Wakpá (Whitewater River)
Ičápšiŋpšiŋčadaŋ Wakpádaŋ (Shallow River)
Ȟé Wašté Wakpá (Eau Galle River)
Bdé Ȟé Wašté (Eau Galle Lake)
Mayá Šá Wakpá (Rush River)
Sápa Wakpá (Black River)
Ȟaȟá Sápa (Black River Falls)

Illustrated by Marlena Myles – Translation by Dawí

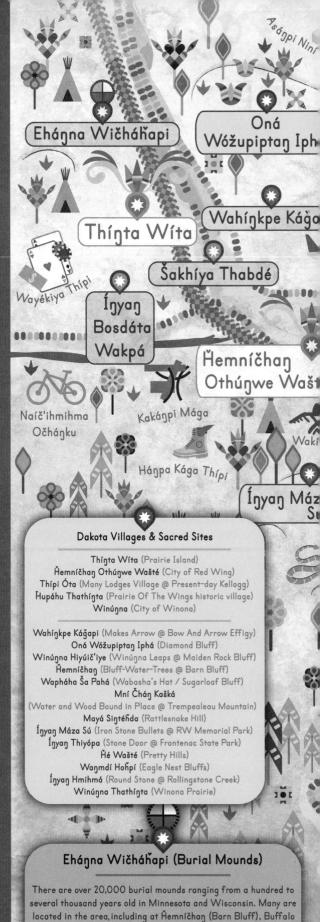

Dakota Villages & Sacred Sites

Thíŋta Wíta (Prairie Island)
Ȟemníčhaŋ Othúŋwe Wašté (City of Red Wing)
Thípi Óta (Many Lodges Village @ Present-day Kellogg)
Ȟupáhu Thathíŋta (Prairie Of The Wings historic village)
Winúŋna (City of Winona)

Wahíŋkpe Káǧapi (Makes Arrow @ Bow And Arrow Effigy)
Oná Wóžupiptaŋ Iphá (Diamond Bluff)
Winúŋna Hiyúič'iye (Winúŋna Leaps @ Maiden Rock Bluff)
Ȟemníčhaŋ (Bluff-Water-Trees @ Barn Bluff)
Wapháha Ša Pahá (Wabasha's Hat / Sugarloaf Bluff)
Mní Čháŋ Kašká (Water and Wood Bound in Place @ Trempealeau Mountain)
Mayá Siŋtéȟda (Rattlesnake Hill)
Íŋyaŋ Máza Sú (Iron Stone Bullets @ RW Memorial Park)
Íŋyaŋ Thiyópa (Stone Door @ Frontenac State Park)
Ȟé Wašté (Pretty Hills)
Waŋmdí Hoȟpí (Eagle Nest Bluffs)
Íŋyaŋ Hmihmá (Round Stone @ Rollingstone Creek)
Winúŋna Thathíŋta (Winona Prairie)

Ehánŋa Wičháȟapi (Burial Mounds)

There are over 20,000 burial mounds ranging from a hundred to several thousand years old in Minnesota and Wisconsin. Many are located in the area, including at Ȟemníčhaŋ (Barn Bluff), Buffalo Slough, and Mní Čháŋ Kašká (Trempealeau Mountain).

Dakhóta Thamákhoče

Thíŋta Wíta · Hemníčhaŋ Othúŋwe Wašté · Winúŋna

Prairie Island · Red Wing · Winona

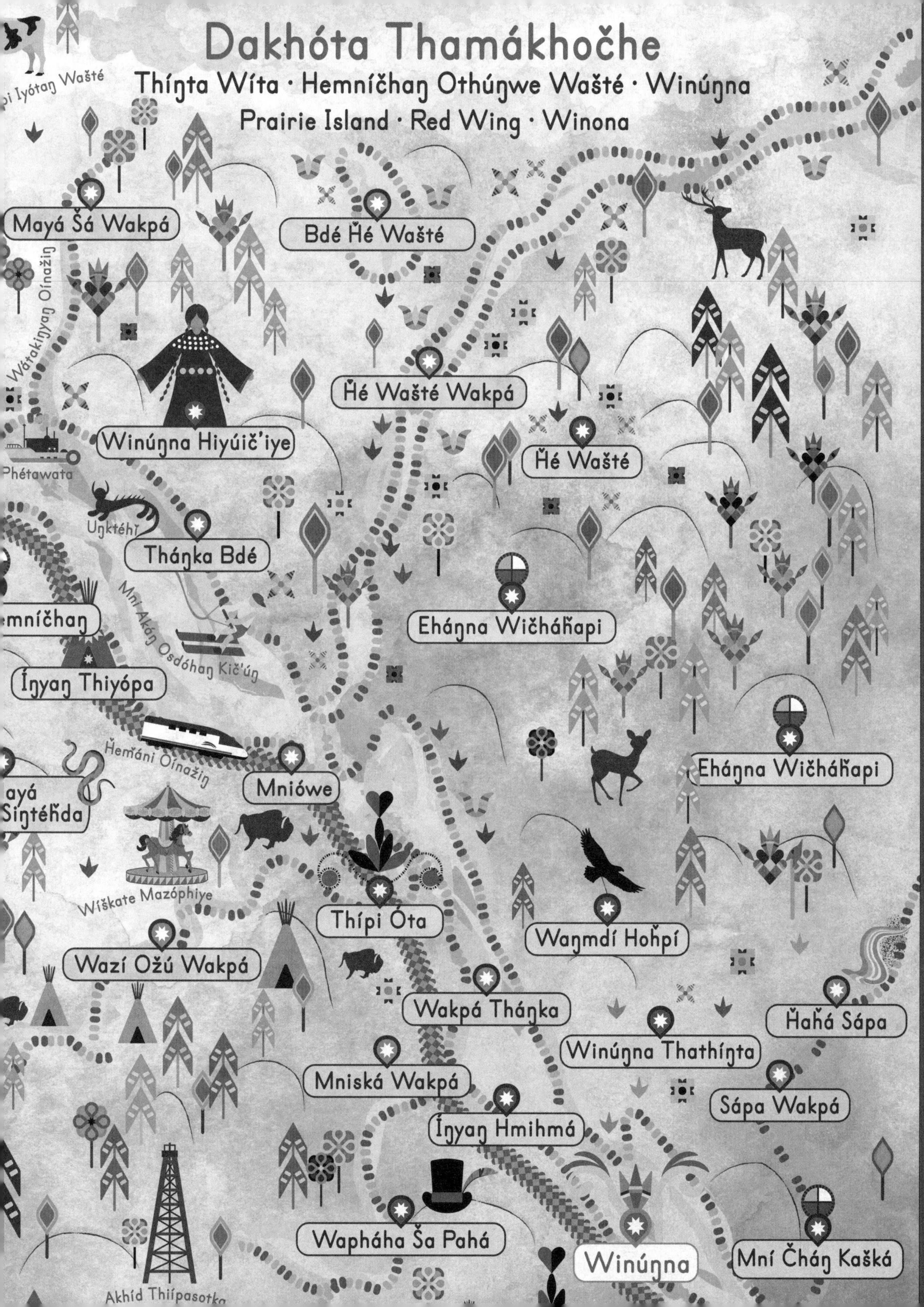

pi Iyótaŋ Wašté
Mayá Šá Wakpá
Bdé Ȟé Wašté
Wátakiŋyaŋ Oínažiŋ
Winúŋna Hiyúič'iye
Phétawata
Ȟé Wašté Wakpá
Ȟé Wašté
Uŋktéȟi
Tháŋka Bdé
Mni Akáŋ Osdóhaŋ Kič'úŋ
Eháŋna Wičháȟapi
mníčhaŋ
Íŋyaŋ Thiyópa
Eháŋna Wičháȟapi
Ȟemáni Oínažiŋ
Mniówe
ayá
Siŋtéȟda
Wiškate Mazóphiye
Thípi Óta
Waŋmdí Hoȟpí
Wazí Ožú Wakpá
Wakpá Tháŋka
Ȟaȟá Sápa
Winúŋna Thathíŋta
Mniská Wakpá
Sápa Wakpá
Íŋyaŋ Hmihmá
Wapháha Ša Pahá
Winúŋna
Mní Čháŋ Kašká
Akhíd Thiípasotka

As people of the woodlands, we have accumulated deep knowledge about plants and trees. They are employed in similar ways by different tribes, so here are just a few of the many plants and some of their uses.

IMPORTANT PLANTS & TREES

From Culturally Important Plants of the Lakota ©1998 Linda S. Black Elk & Sitting Bull College.

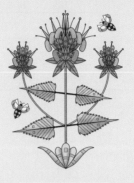

Bee Balm

Used in a variety of preparations to treat fevers, indigestion, sore throats, colds, whooping cough, fainting, and snakebite.

Stinging Nettles

Excellent for treating inflammation. A decoction of the young leaves is ingested to treat hives, and an infusion is used to treat arthritis, rheumatism, and eczema.

Cudleaf Sage

The leaves and stems are burned as incense for "smudging," a practice where smoke from the plant is breathed in and wafted all over the body to purify oneself.

Eastern Red Cedar

Inhaling smoke from burning twigs relieves head congestion. A decoction made from the leaves and cones is used to relieve coughing.

Coneflower

A tincture made from the root can relieve flu and cold symptoms. Chewing the roots relieves tonsillitis, toothaches, stomachaches, and sore throats and quenches thirst.

Goldenrod

A decoction of the whole plant is used to aid in expelling kidney stones, and poultices of the root are applied to soothe burns.

Prairie Rose

The hips contain essential fatty acids and high levels of Vitamin C. They can be dried and saved for later consumption, especially during periods of food scarcity.

A bright light: Indigenous food is making a spectacular comeback, thanks to people like Sean Sherman and his Indigenous restaurant, Owamni. An Oglala Lakota Sioux, Sherman—who grew up on a reservation and learned to forage for local foods from his grandparents—is now one of America's most lauded chefs and cookbook authors. In a recent profile in *The New Yorker*, Sherman, who serves dishes made without wheat flour, dairy, cane sugar, or any other ingredient brought in by Europeans, said, "The diet of our ancestors, it was almost a perfect diet. It's what the paleo diet wants to be: gluten-free, dairy-free, sugar-free."

Sean Sherman at the Tatanka Truck

ABOUT THE AUTHORS

NOAH VAN SCIVER is an award-winning cartoonist who grew up in a Mormon family in New Jersey. As far back as he remembers, he always loved the Paul Bunyan story and was eager to find out more about its origins. He was amused when he found out that William B. Laughead, the story's creator, was a cartoonist as well as an advertising man. Van Sciver is the author of critically acclaimed and best-selling graphic novels, including *One Dirty Tree*, the Fante Bukowski: Struggling Writer series, and *Joseph Smith and the Mormons*. He has received mutiple Eisner nominations and was a regular contributor to *MAD Magazine*. He currently resides in Columbia, South Carolina, with his wife and child.

MARLENA MYLES is a self-taught Native American (Spirit Lake Dakota/Mohegan/Muscogee) artist who grew up on her traditional Dakota homelands. Her work includes children's books, murals, fabrics, and augmented reality. Her fine art has been shown in places like the Minneapolis Institute of Art, the Red Cloud Heritage Center, and the Minnesota Museum of American Art, to name a few. She enjoys using the land as a teacher to share with Minnesotans of all backgrounds the Indigenous history of this place we all call home. She runs her own Dakota publishing company, Wíyouŋkihipi (We Are Capable) Productions, to create a wider platform that educates and honors the culture, language, and history of Dakota people. She currently lives in St. Paul, Minnesota.

DR. INDIGINERD a.k.a. **LEE FRANCIS IV** is the Executive Director of Native Realities, an Indigenous imagination organization that seeks to engage and inspire Indigenous youth and communities through pop culture media and culturally dynamic programming. Dr. Francis also founded the Indigenous Comic Con (now IndigiPop Expo) and opened Red Planet Books and Comics, the first Native comic shop in the world, in 2017. He received his PhD in Education from Texas State University and currently resides in North Carolina with his family.

DR. DEONDRE SMILES is an assistant professor in the Department of Geography at the University of Victoria, BC, Canada. He is of Ojibwe, Black, and Swedish descent and is a proud citizen of the Leech Lake Band of Ojibwe. Dr. Smiles's interests are many and include Indigenous geographies, human-environment interactions, and Indigenous cultural resource management and preservation. He serves as the principal investigator for the Geographic Indigenous Futures Collaboratory, one of Western Canada's first Indigenous geographies-focused labs.

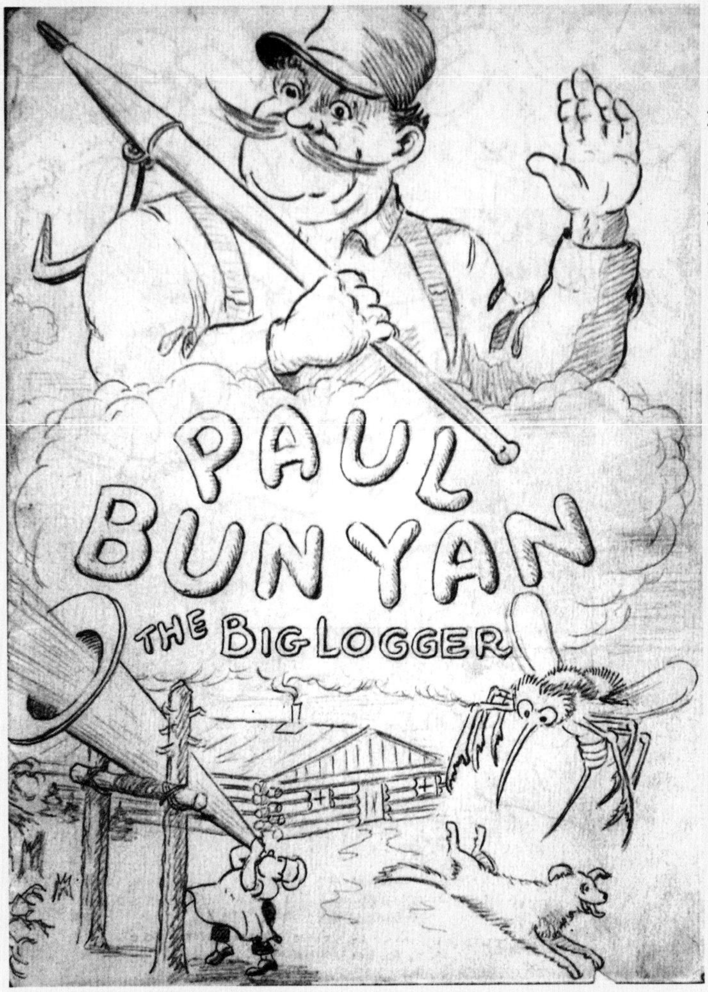
PAUL
BUNYAN
THE BIG LOGGER

Original Paul Bunyan sketches by W. B. Laughead. Courtesy: Kerlan Collection, University of Minnesota Libraries.

Bibliography – Further Reading

The Marvelous Exploits of Paul Bunyan. W. B. Laughead. Kessinger Publishing, LLC, 2010. *One of Laughead's many pamphlets that popularized Paul Bunyan.*

Nenaboozhoo and Paul Bunyan. Dr. Giniwgiizhig, Zhaawanwewindamook (translator), and Anna Granholm (illustrator). Black Bears and Blueberries, 2022. *An illustrated Ojibwe story featuring Anishinaabe legend Nenaboozhoo facing off against Paul Bunyan. Ages 4-6*

Moonshot: The Indigenous Comics Collection. (Vol. 3). Elizabeth LaPensée and Michael Sheyahshe (editors). Inhabit Education Books Inc., 2020. *A collection of comics written by Native authors. Ages 10+*

Trickster: Native American Tales, A Graphic Collection. Edited by Matt Dembicki. Chicago Review Press, 2021. *A collection of stories written by Native authors. Ages 12+*

Trick of the Tale: A Collection of Trickster Tales. John Matthews, Caitlín Matthews, and Tomislav Tomić (Illustrator). Candlewick, 2008. *A collection of trickster tales spanning the globe — including several Native American stories. Ages 12+*

Paul Bunyan. Esther Shephard and Rockwell Kent (illustrator). Clarion Books, 2006. *One of the earliest and most influential collections of classic Bunyan tall tales, originally published in 1924. Ages 7-10.*

Legends of Paul Bunyan. Harold W. Felton (editor). University of Minnesota Press, 1947. *A selection of works by more than 30 authors (including Laughead and Robert Frost) on Paul Bunyan. Ages 8+*

The Legend of Auntie Po. Shing Yin Khor. Kokila, 2021. *The Paul Bunyan character reimagined as a Chinese-American heroine. Ages 10+*

Out of the Northwoods: The Many Lives of Paul Bunyan. Michael Edmonds. Wisconsin Historical Society Press, 2009. *A historical overview of the Bunyan character, including eyewitness accounts from loggers.*

Online Resources:

AMERICANFOLKLORE.NET
Retelling of folktales, myths, and legends from all over the Americas.

AMERICANINDIANSINCHILDRENSLITERATURE.BLOGSPOT.COM
American Indians in Children's Literature (AICL) provides critical analysis of Indigenous peoples in children's and young adult books.

LIBGUIDES.MNSU.EDU
A multiculturally grounded guide to finding Native American Children's and Young Adult Literature.